CONTENTS

Marion Foale

KNITTING COLLECTION

BOOK ONE

Marion Foale Des R.C.A. is one of Britain's most respected fashion designers.

Whilst a student at the Royal College of Art, Marion achieved the honour of having her design chosen for the Queen's Mantle worn for the annual Order of the British Empire's dedication ceremony.

At the start of the Swinging Sixties and, on attaining their degrees in 1961, Marion and Sally Tuffin started their own business, Foale and Tuffin. In 1963 they launched one of Carnaby Street's trendiest boutiques catering for the fashion conscious young woman of the day.

From 1965 to 1970 Foale and Tuffin signed for Youth Quake together with Mary Quant and Betsy Johnson embarking on whistle stop tours around the U.S.A. with Go Go girls to model and a boy band called The Skunks bashing out the sounds. During 1966, they designed the clothes worn in the films Kaleidoscope, starring Susannah York and Warren Beatty, and Two For The Road with Audrey Hepburn and Albert Finney.

In 1972, Marion settled into family life in a 16th Century thatched farmhouse on the Warwickshire borders. By 1981 she realized there was a desire for quality hand knitwear so, with this in mind, and working from home, she set about designing her own collection. Using her previous experience in fashion design, she developed a new method of styling knitwear into tailored, structured shapes with an imaginative use of traditional stitches. Thus, she began creating classic and fashion styles, suitable for a wide range of customers. Her garments have become famous for their craftsmanship and perfect attention to detail and finish. Marion has always believed that only the best will do, and so has developed her own exclusive brand of 3 ply wool.

Now working with eight permanent staff from studio premises in a local historic market town, Foale Ltd is famous as an international fashion business, selling Marion's exclusive range of garments to customers around the world. Approximately three hundred local hand knitters are busily knitting to order with a separate group hand sewing and finishing each piece.

In 2009, a retrospective exhibition titled *Foale and Tuffin—Made in England* was held at the Fashion and Textile Museum in London. Iain R. Webb's book *Foale and Tuffin: The Sixties. A Decade in Fashion* was published to coincide with this exhibition.

I realize with some degree of amazement that it has been 25 years since I last organized a collection exclusively for hand knitters—and nearly 50 years since my career began in fashion design. It is with great pleasure that I embark on my new passion to share designs from my extensive pattern archive with you.

Marion Foale

6

ALICIA •••••

12

ARRAN •••

18

CLOCHE ••

22

DIAMOND ••••

30

CRYSTAL •

34

ISOBEL •••

EASY •
EASY/MEDIUM ••
MEDIUM •••
MEDIUM/DIFFICULT ••••
DIFFICULT •••••

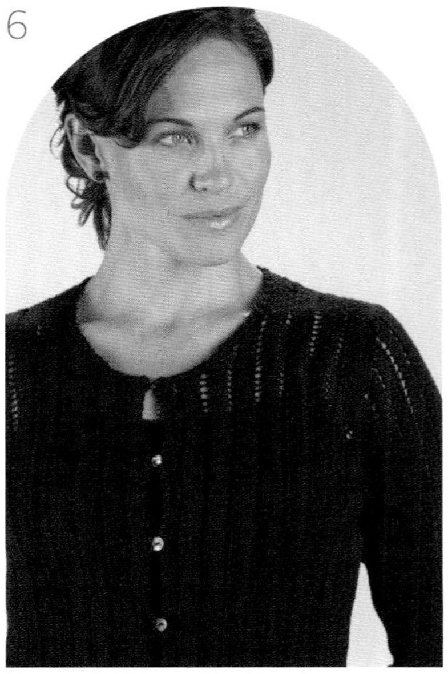

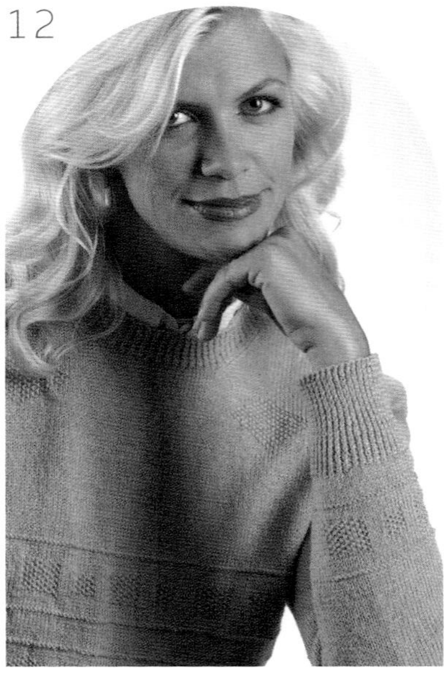

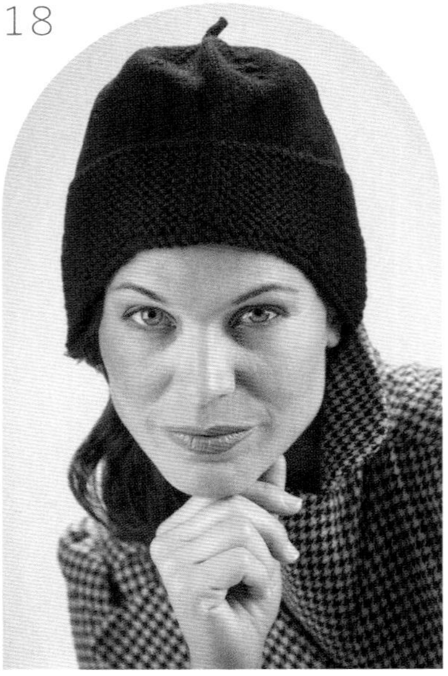

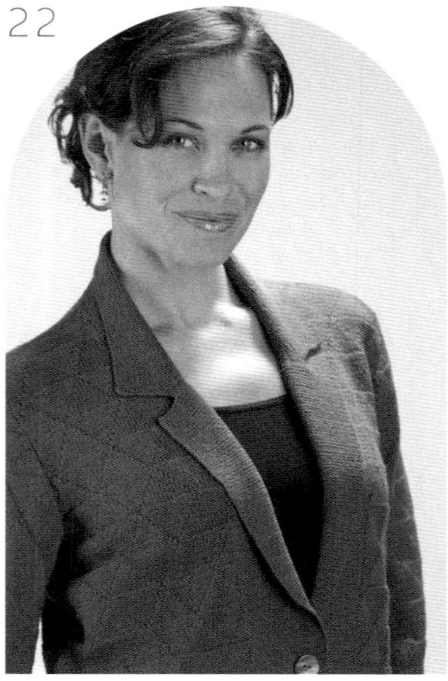

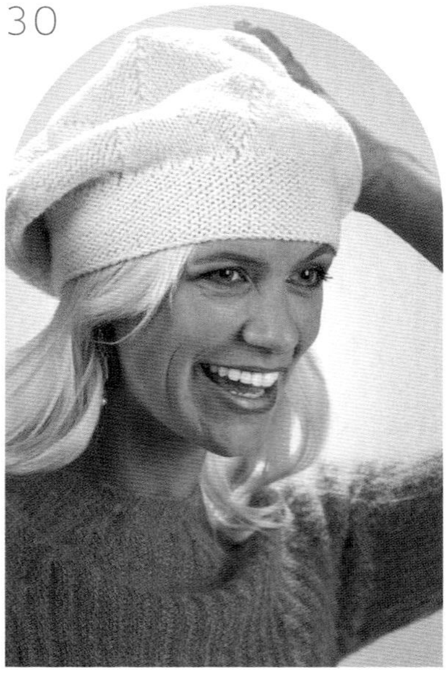

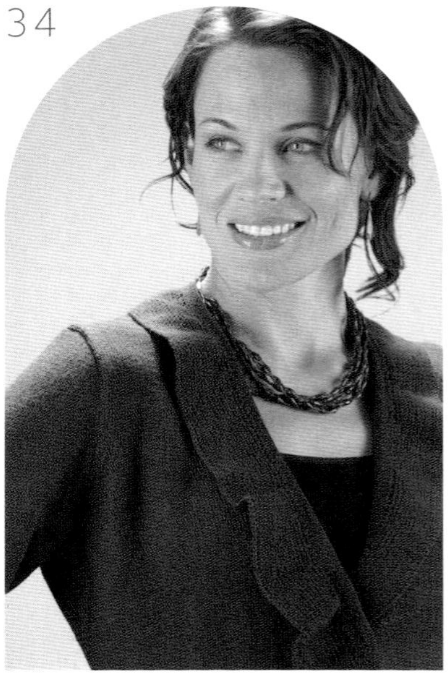

ALICIA

MEASUREMENTS

The body is knitted in a lace stitch that gives to fit a range of measurements.

To Fit Bust Size: 32–36" (38–42")
Finished Length: 26½" (27")
Sleeve Length —*seam*: 17" (17")

MATERIALS

Yarn: 400 (450) grams **Marion Foale 3ply Wool** —*8 (9) 50g balls.* Shown in Cream #004 and Black #001

- Pair size 6 (4 mm) needles
- Pair size 3 (3¼ mm) needles
- 7 buttons to fit worked loop

GAUGE

On size 6 (4 mm) needles in St st,
26 sts & 38 rows = 4" square

BACK

Using **size 6 (4 mm) needles**, CO 193 (217) sts.

⊙
Row 1 (RS): Work Edging: Work 2 rows knit.
Row 3: K1, * yo, k2tog, rep from * to end of row.

Work 1 row knit.

Row 5: Join tog with CO edge as follows: * K1, k next st with 2nd st of cast on edge to make 1 st, rep from * to last st, k1.
Make sure you have always worked together corresponding sts from CO edge so that hem is not twisted.
Row 6 (WS): Work 1 row purl.
⊙

⊙⊙⊙
Now work **3 rows of holes** as follows:

Row 1 (RS): K1, * yo, k2tog, rep from * to end of row.
Row 2 *and alternate rows*: Purl.
Row 3: K2, * yo, k2tog, rep from * to last st, k1.
Row 5: As first row.
Row 6: As set.
Work 2 rows St st —8 rows

⊙⊙⊙⊙
Now work **DIAMOND PATTERN** as follows:

Row 1 (RS): * K4, k2tog tbl, yo, k1, yo, k2tog, k3, rep from * to last st, k1.
Row 2 *and alternate rows*: Purl.
Row 3: * K3, k2tog tbl, yo, k3, yo, k2tog, k2, rep from * to last st, k1.
Row 5: * K2, k2tog tbl, yo, k5, yo, k2tog, k1, rep from * to last st, k1.
Row 7: * K1, k2tog tbl, yo, k7, yo, k2tog, rep from * to last st, k1.
Row 9: * K1, yo, k2tog, k7, k2tog tbl, yo, rep from * to last st, k1.
Row 11: * K2, yo, k2tog, k5, k2tog tbl, yo, k1, rep from * to last st, k1.
Row 13: * K3, yo, k2tog, k3, k2tog tbl, yo, k2, rep from * to last st, k1.
Row 15: * K4, yo, k2tog, k1, k2tog tbl, yo, k3, rep from * to last st, k1.
Row 17: * K4, k2tog tbl, yo, k1, yo, k2tog, k3, rep from * to last st, k1.
Row 18: Purl as set.
These last 18 rows complete Diamond Pattern.

Work 1 row knit.
⊙⊙⊙

WORK 1ST DEC ROW as follows: **(WS)**: P1 (1), * p2tog, p2 (* p2tog, p2, p2tog, p3), rep from * to end of row —145 (169) sts

Now work from ⊙⊙⊙ to ⊙⊙⊙ for 3 rows of holes and second Diamond Pattern.

WORK 2ND DEC ROW (WS): P2 (4), * p2tog, p4, p2tog, p3, rep from * to end of row —119 (139 sts)

This completes the 2 tiered peplum.

Now work **BODICE** in **STRIPE PATTERN** as follows:

Row 1 (RS): K1, * k8, yo, k2tog, rep from * to last 8 sts, k to end of row.
Row 2 *and alternate rows*: Purl.
Repeat these last 2 rows 3 more times.

Row 9: K3, * k2tog tbl, yo, k4, yo, k2tog, k2, rep from * to last 6 sts, k2tog tbl, yo, k4.
Row 10 *and alternate rows*: Purl.
These last 2 rows set the pattern.

Cont as set to work a further 78 rows —90 rows

SHAPE ARMHOLES

Row 1 (RS): Cont in Stripe Pattern as set, BO 7 sts at beg of next 2 rows —105 (125) sts

Now dec 1 st at each end of 3rd and then RS rows working pattern as number of sts allows until 83 (99) sts rem.

Now work straight as follows:

WS: Purl.
RS: K5 (3), * k2tog tbl, yo, k4, yo, k2tog, k2, rep from * to last 8 (6) sts, k2tog tbl, yo, k6 (4).
These 2 rows set the pattern.

Cont as set to work a further 33 (39) rows —56 (66) rows

SHAPE NECK

Next Row (RS): Work 34 (40) sts, turn, cont on these sts dec 1 st at neck edge every following row, when 5 dec have been worked —29 (35) sts —62 (72) rows

SHAPE SHOULDER

Next Row (RS): Cont neck edge dec as set, *AT THE SAME TIME*, BO 7 (9) sts at the beg of this and alternate row, work 1 row, BO rem sts, rejoin yarn, BO centre 15 (19) sts, work rem 34 (40) sts to match.

LEFT FRONT

Using **size 6 (4 mm) needles**, CO 94 (106) sts.

Row 1 (RS): WORK EDGING: Work 2 rows knit.
Row 3: K1, * yo, k2tog, rep from * to last 3 sts, k3.

Work 1 row knit.

Row 5: Join tog with cast on edge as follows: * K1, k next st with 2nd st of cast on edge to make 1 st, rep from * to end of row.
Row 6 (WS): Work 1 row purl.

⊙⊙
Now work **3 rows of holes** as follows:

Row 1 (RS): K1, * yo, k2tog, rep from * to last 3 sts, k3.
Row 2 *and alternate rows*: Purl.
Row 3: K2, * yo, k2tog, rep from * to last 2 sts, k2.
Row 5: As first row.
Row 6: As set.

Work 2 rows St st —8 rows

Now work **DIAMOND PATTERN** as follows:

Row 1 (RS): * K4, k2tog tbl, yo, k1, yo, k2tog, k3, rep from * to last 10 sts, k4, k2tog tbl, yo, k4.
Row 2 *and alternate rows*: Purl.
Row 3: * K3, k2tog tbl, yo, k3, yo, k2tog, k2, rep from * to last 10 sts, k3, k2tog tbl, yo, k5.
Row 5: * K2, k2tog tbl, yo, k5, yo, k2tog, k1, rep from * to last 10 sts, k2, k2tog tbl, yo, k6.
Row 7: * K1, k2tog tbl, yo, k7, yo, k2tog, rep from * to last 10 sts, k1, k2tog tbl, yo, k7.
Row 9: * K1, yo, k2tog, k7, k2tog tbl, yo, rep from * to last 10 sts, k1, yo, k2tog, k7.
Row 11: * K2, yo, k2tog, k5, k2tog tbl, yo, k1, rep from * to last 10 sts, k2, yo, k2tog, k6.
Row 13: * K3, yo, k2tog, k3, k2tog tbl, yo, k2, rep from * to last 10 sts, k3, yo, k2tog, k5.
Row 15: * K4, yo, k2tog, k1, k2tog tbl, yo, k3, rep from * to last 10 sts, k4, yo, k2tog, k4.
Row 17: * K4, k2tog tbl, yo, k1, yo, k2tog, k3, rep from * to last 10 sts, k4, k2tog tbl, yo, k4.
Row 18: Purl as set.
These last 18 rows complete Diamond Pattern.

Work 1 row knit.
⊙⊙

WORK 1ST DEC ROW (WS): P0 (6), * p2tog, p2, rep from * to last 2 (4) sts, p2tog (p4) —70 (82) sts

Now work from ⊙⊙ to ⊙⊙.

WORK 2ND DEC ROW as follows: **(WS):** P0 (0), * p2, p2tog, p3, rep from * to last 4 (4) sts, p2tog, p2 —58 (68) sts

This completes the 2 tiered peplum.

Now work **BODICE** in **STRIPE PATTERN** as follows:

Row 1 (RS): K1, * k8, yo, k2tog, rep from * to last 7 sts, k to end of row.
Row 2 *and alternate rows*: Purl.
Repeat these last 2 rows 3 more times.

Row 9: K3, * k2tog tbl, yo, k4, yo, k2tog, k2, rep from * to last 5 sts, k2tog tbl, yo, k3.
Row 10 *and alternate rows*: Purl.
These last 2 rows set the pattern.

Cont as set to work 80 rows – *90 rows*

SHAPE ARMHOLE

Row 1 (RS): BO 7 sts, work to end of row in Stripe Pattern as set – *51 (61) sts*
Now dec 1 st at armhole edge on RS rows working pattern as number of sts allows until 40 (48) sts rem.

Work 5 (5) rows – *28 (32) rows*

SHAPE NECK

Next Row (RS): Work as set.
Next Row: BO first 7 sts, p to end of row – *33 (41) sts*

Now dec 1 st at neck edge on next and then RS rows until 23 (29) sts rem, work 13 (15) rows keeping continuity of pattern as set as number of sts allows – *62 (72) rows*

SHAPE SHOULDER

Next Row (RS): BO 7 (9) sts at the beg of this and then alternate row, work 1 row, BO rem sts.

RIGHT FRONT

Work the same as Left Front, REVERSING *Shaping and Pattern* as follows:

Edging: **Row 3 (RS):** K3, * yo, k2tog, rep from * to last st, k1.

3 Rows of Holes:
Row 1 (RS): K4, * yo, k2tog, rep from * to end of row.
Row 3: K3, * yo, k2tog, rep from * to last st, k1.

Diamond Pattern:
Row 1 (RS): K4, yo, k2tog, k3, * k4, k2tog tbl, yo, k1, yo, k2tog, k3, rep from * to last st, k1.
Row 3: K5, yo, k2tog, k2, * k3, k2tog tbl, yo, k3, yo, k2tog, k2, rep from * to last st, k1.
Row 5: K6, yo, k2tog, k1, * k2, k2tog tbl, yo, k5, yo, k2tog, k1, rep from * to last st, k1.
This sets the position of the pattern.

Work 1st Dec Row **WS:** As Left Front.
Work 2nd Dec Row **WS:** As Left Front.

Stripe Pattern for Bodice:
Row 1 (RS): * K8, yo, k2tog, rep from * to last 8 sts, k8.
Row 9: * K2, k2tog tbl, yo, k4, yo, k2tog, rep from * to last 8 sts, k2, k2tog tbl, yo, k4.

Shape Armhole:
Row 1 (RS): Work as set
Row 2: BO first 7 sts, p to end of row – *51 (61) sts*

Shape Neck:
Next Row (RS): BO first 7 sts, work to end of row – *33 (43) sts*

NECK EDGE

Use **size 3 (3¼ mm) needles. RS:** Starting with right front

pick up and knit 6 sts from BO sts, 30 (34) sts (approx 3 sts from every 4 rows) up side front, 11 sts down side back, (1 st from each row), 13 (17) sts from BO back neck, 11 sts up side back, 30 (34) sts down side front and 6 sts from BO sts *—107 (119) sts*

Row 1 (WS): <u>WORK EDGING:</u> Work 1 row knit.

Next Row (RS): K1, * yo, k2tog, rep from * to end of row.

Work 2 rows knit *— 4 rows*

Using a **size 6 (4 mm) needle,** BO in k1, p1 to give with knitting.

FRONT EDGE

WORK 2 THE SAME

Use **size 3 (3¼ mm) needles. RS:** With edging hem turned up at both bottom edge and neck edge, pick up and knit 1 st from edging at hem, 123 (127) sts along front edge (approx 5 sts from every 7 rows) and 1 st from edging at neck edge *—125 (129) sts*

Row 1 (WS): <u>WORK EDGING:</u> Work 1 row knit.

Next Row (RS): K1, * yo, k2tog, rep from * to last st, k1.

Work 2 rows knit *—4 rows*

Using **a size 6 (4 mm) needle,** BO in k1, p1 *(to give with knitting).*

SLEEVES

WORK 2 THE SAME

Using **size 6 (4 mm) needles,** CO 55 (65) sts. Work **Edging** as given for Back from ⊙ to ⊙.

Now work **3 rows of holes** as given for Back from ⊙⊙⊙ to ⊙⊙⊙⊙.

Now cont in **<u>STRIPE PATTERN</u>** as follows:

Row 1 (RS): K7, * yo, k2tog, k8, rep from * to last 8 sts, yo, k2tog, k6.
Row 2 *and alternate rows*: Purl.
Repeat these last 2 rows 3 more times.

Row 9 (RS): K1, k2tog tbl, yo, k4, * yo, k2tog, k2, k2tog tbl, yo, k4, rep from * to last 8 sts, yo, k2tog, k2, k2tog tbl, yo, k2.
Row 10 *and alternate rows*: Purl.
These last 2 rows set the pattern.

Cont as set inc 1 st at each end of the 28th and then following 6th rows (WS) keeping pattern correct as number of sts allows.

When there are 91 (101) sts, work 10 rows *— 140 rows*

SHAPE TOP

RS: Cont in pattern as set, BO 7 sts at the beg of next 2 rows *—77 (87) sts*

Now dec 1 st at each end on next and then alternate rows until 55 (61) sts rem.

Now dec 1 st at each end of every row until 19 (23) sts rem. BO.

SEWING UP

Work in all ends, sew side seams, shoulder seams and sleeve seams. Fold and sew front BO edges to WS to look the same as bottom edging. Then work the same at neck edge. Mark positions and sew 7 buttons on bodice section, now work or crochet 7 loops to match positions. Set sleeves to armholes, (centre of sleeve to shoulder seam).

We advise you to dry clean this garment as the open knit is very stretchy when washed.

ARRAN

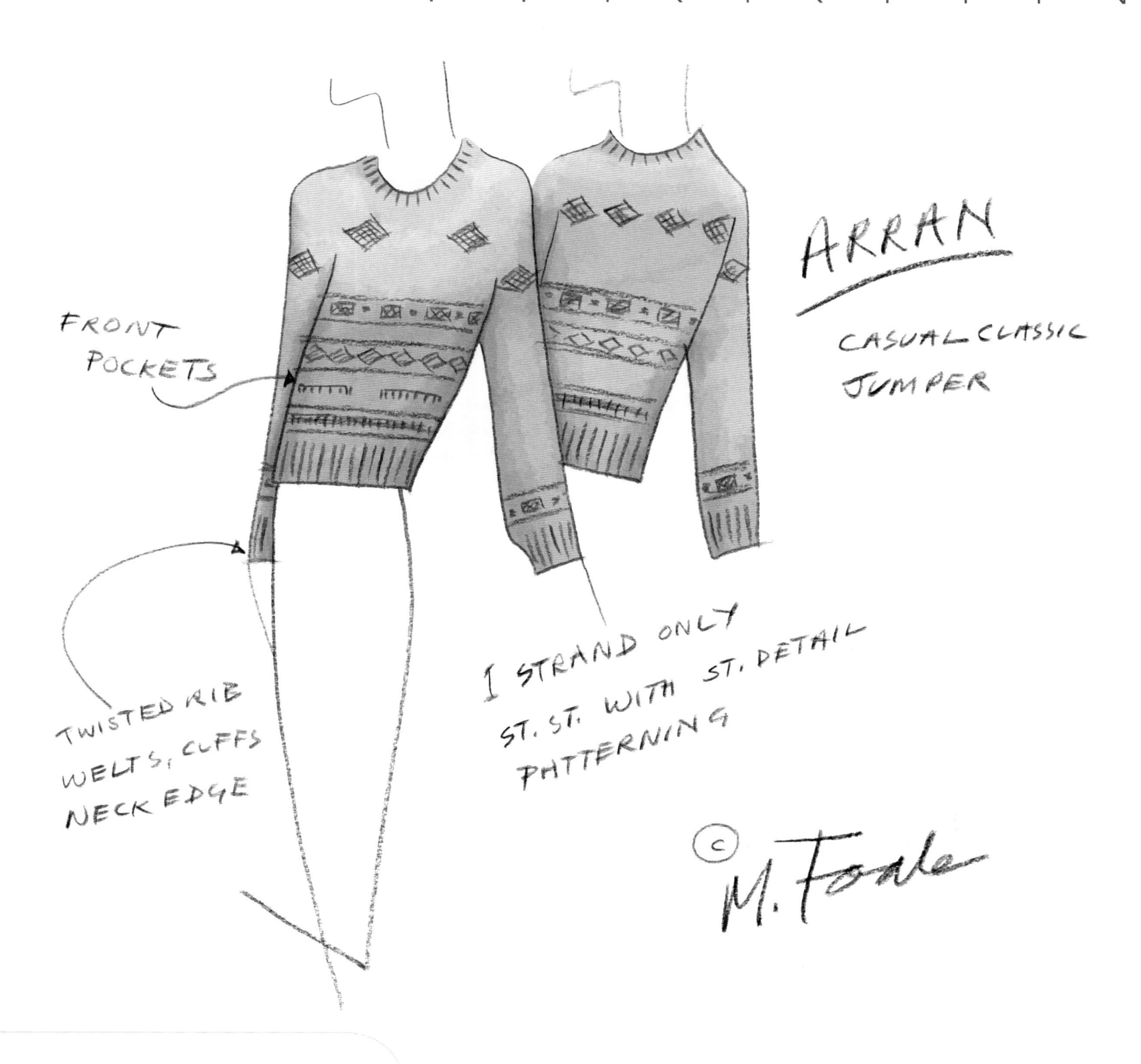

MEASUREMENTS

Actual Measurement at Chest: 39" (44½")
Finished Length: 23½"
Sleeve Length —*Seam*: 18"

MATERIALS

- Pair size 1 (2¼ mm) needles
- Pair size 2 (3 mm) needles
- Pair size 2 (2¾ mm) needles
- Circular needle size 1 (2¼ mm) needles

Yarn: 450 (550) grams **Marion Foale 3ply Wool** —*9 (11) 50g balls*. Shown in color Ashrose #048.

GAUGE

On size 2 (3 mm) needles in St st.
32 sts & 42 rows = 4" square

BACK

⊙⊙

Using **size 1 (2¼ mm) needles**, CO 178 (201) sts. Now work in k1, p1 twisted rib (k into back of k st). Work 32 rows in all.

Change to **size 2 (3 mm) needles.**
Row 1 (RS): K1 (0), (k3, k2tog, k3) 22 (25) times, k1 (1) *— 156 (176) sts*

Work 9 rows St st.

Row 11 (RS): Purl
Now work 3 rows St st starting WS with a p row.

Change to **size 2 (2¾ mm) needles** and work **CHECK PATTERN** as follows:
Row 15 (RS): (k2, p2) 39 (44) times.
Row 16: (k2, p2) 39 (44) times.
Row 17: (p2, k2) 39 (44) times.
Row 18: (p2, k2) 39 (44) times.
These last 4 rows set the pattern.

Cont repeating to work 16 rows in all, ending last row as follows: dec 1 st (inc 1 st)
—155 (177) sts

Change to **size 2 (3 mm) needles.**
Row 31 (RS): Starting with a k row, work 3 rows St st.
Row 34 (WS): Knit.
This completes the Check Pattern.

Row 35 (RS): Starting with a k row, work 28 rows St st.

Now work **SMALL DIAMOND PATTERN** as follows:
Row 63 (RS): Purl.
Now work 3 rows St st starting WS with a p row.

Row 67: (k11, p1, k10) 7 (8) times, k1.
Row 68: P1, (p9, k1, p1, k1, p10) 7 (8) times.
Row 69: [k9 (p1, k1) twice, p1, k8] 7 (8) times, k1.
Row 70: P1, [p7 (k1, p1) 3 times, k1, p8] 7 (8) times.
Row 71: [k7 (p1, k1) 4 times, p1, k6] 7 (8) times, k1.
Row 72: P1, [p5 (k1, p1) 5 times, k1, p6] 7 (8) times.
Row 73: [k5 (p1, k1) 6 times, p1, k4] 7 (8) times, k1.
Row 74: P1, [p3 (k1, p1) 7 times, k1, p4] 7 (8) times.

Now work diamond in reverse starting as follows:
Row 75: As row 73.
Row 76: As row 72.
This sets the pattern.

When 81 rows have been worked, the diamonds are complete.

Row 82 (WS): Starting with a p row, work 3 rows St st.
Row 85 (RS): Purl.
These last 22 rows complete the Small Diamond Pattern.

Row 86 (WS): Starting with a p row, work 9 rows St st.

Now work **SQUARES PATTERN** as follows:
Row 95 (RS): Purl.
Now work 5 rows St st starting WS with a p row.

Row 101: [k7 (p1, k1) 4 times, p1, k6] 7 (8) times, k1.
Row 102: P1 [p7 (k1, p1) 4 times, p7] 7 (8) times.
Row 103: [p1, k1, p1, k4 (p1, k1) 4 times, p1, k4, p1, k1] 7 (8) times, p1.
Row 104: P1[k1, p6 (k1, p1) 3 times, k1, p6, k1, p1], 7 (8) times.

Rows 105, 107, & 109: As row 103.
Rows 106 & 108: As row 104.
Row 110: As row 102.
Row 111: As row 101.

Starting WS with a p row, work 5 rows St st.
Row 117 (RS): Purl.
These last 22 rows complete the Squares Pattern.

Starting WS with a p row, work 11 rows St st —128 rows in all from welt.

SHAPE ARMHOLES

Row 1 (RS): Cont in St st, binding off first 8 sts of this and next row —139 (161) sts

Now dec 1 st at each end of the next and then following alternate rows until 115 (133) sts. Work 1 row.

⊙⊙⊙
Now work **LARGE DIAMOND PATTERN** as follows:
Row 1 (RS): K8 (17), (k10, p1, k15) 4 (4) times, k3 (12).
Row 2: P3 (12), (p14, k1, p1, k1, p9) 4 (4) times, p8 (17).
Row 3: K8 (17), [k8, (p1, k1) twice, p1, k13] 4 (4) times, k3 (12).
Row 4: P3 (12), [p12, (k1, p1) 3 times, k1, p7] 4 (4) times, p8 (17).
Row 5: K8 (17), [k6 (p1, k1) 4 times, p1, k11] 4 (4) times, k3 (12).
Row 6: P3 (12), [p10, (k1, p1) 5 times, k1, p5] 4 (4) times, p8 (17).
This sets the pattern.

Cont as set inc each diamond by 2 sts every row until 11th row is worked (21 sts in moss as established for each diamond).

Now work diamonds in reverse as follows:
Row 12: As row 10.
Row 13: As row 9.
Cont as set.

When 21 rows have been worked, diamonds are complete —47 (51) rows from shape armholes

Starting WS with a p row, work 31 (39) rows in St st —78 (90) rows

SHAPE SHOULDERS, SHAPE NECK

Row 1 (RS): BO first 8 (10) sts at beg of this and next row —99 (113) sts, k30 (35), turn, cont on these sts dec 1 st at neck edge every following row (not fully fashioned). *AT THE SAME TIME,* on the 3rd and 5th rows, BO first 8 (10) sts, work as set to end of row. Work 1 row, BO rem sts, leave centre 39 (43) sts on a ssth. Rejoin yarn, and work rem 30 (35) sts to match, binding off shoulder sts on 4th, 6th and 8th rows.

POCKET LINING

WORK 2 THE SAME

Using **size 2 (3 mm) needles,** CO 40 sts. Work 42 rows St st leave sts on a ssth.

FRONT

Work the same as Back from ⊙⊙, *AT THE SAME TIME* when 44 rows have been worked, place pocket linings as follows:

Row 45 (RS): PLACE POCKET LININGS: K15 (22), slip next 40 sts onto a ssth and in place of these k across 40 sts of pocket lining, k45 (53), slip next 40 sts onto a ssth and in place of these k across other pocket lining, k15 (22).

Now cont as given for back to ⊙⊙⊙.

Now work **LARGE DIAMOND PATTERN** as follows:
Row 1 (RS): K27 (32), p1, k59 (67), p1, k27 (32).
Row 2: P26 (31), k1, p1, k1, p57 (65), k1, p1, k1, p26 (31).
Row 3: K25 (30), (p1, k1) twice, p1, k55 (63), (p1, k1) twice, p1, k25 (30).
Row 4: P24 (29), (k1, p1) 3 times, k1, p53 (61), (k1, p1) 3 times, k1, p24 (29).
Row 5: K23 (28), (p1, k1) 4 times, p1, k51 (59), (p1, k1) 4 times, p1, k23 (28).
Row 6: P22 (27), (k1, p1) 5 times, k1, p49 (57), (k1, p1) 5 times, k1, p22 (27).
This sets the pattern.

Cont as set inc each diamond by 2 sts every row until 11th row is worked.

Now work diamonds in reverse as follows:

Row 12: As row 10.
Row 13: As row 9.
This sets the pattern.

When 21 rows have been worked diamonds are complete.

Work 1 (3) rows – 48 (54) rows

SHAPE NECK

Next Row (RS): K44 (51) sts, turn, cont on these sts dec 1 st at neck edge on the 3rd and then alternate rows as follows:

RS: K to last 5 sts k2tog, k3.

When 33 (40) sts rem, work 7 (13) rows – 78 (90) rows

SHAPE SHOULDER

Next Row (RS): BO next 8 (10) sts at the beg of this and then 2 following alternate rows, work 1 row, BO rem sts.

Leave centre 27 (31) sts on a ssth, rejoin yarn and work rem 44 (51) sts to match, working neck dec as follows:

RS: K3, k2tog tbl, k to end of row.

POCKET TOP

WORK 2 THE SAME

Using **size 1 (2¼ mm) needles**, pick up the 40 sts on ssth and work 10 rows in k1, p1 twisted rib, BO in k1, p1.

NECK EDGE

Using **size 1 (2¼ mm) circular needle** starting at shoulder, pick up and knit 5 sts down side back, 39 (43) sts on ssth, (back neck) 5 sts up side back, 28 (32) sts down side front, (approx 3 sts from every 4 rows), 27 (31) sts on ssth (front neck) and 28 (32) sts up side front – 132 (148) sts

Now work in k1, p1 twisted rib as follows:

ROUND 1: * K1b, p1, rep from * to end of round.
ROUND 2: * K1, p1, rep from * to end of round.

Cont repeating these 2 rounds to work 12 in all, BO in k1, p1 *(make sure it goes over your head).*

SLEEVES

WORK 2 THE SAME

Using **size 1 (2¼ mm) needles**, CO 73 (75) sts. Work 32 rows in k1, p1 twisted rib.

Change to **size 2 (3 mm) needles** and cont in St st inc 1 st at each end of the 5th and 3 following 9th rows as follows:

RS & WS Rows: Work 2, work and inc into next st, work to last 4 sts, work and inc into next st, work 3.

When 10 rows are worked – 75 (77) sts work **SQUARES PATTERN** cont inc rows as set, as follows:
Row 11 (RS): Purl.

Starting WS with a p row, work 5 rows St st.
Row 17: – 77 (79) sts K12 (13), [(p1, k1) 4 times, p1, k13] twice, (p1, k1) 4 times, p1, k12 (13).
Row 18: P13 (14), [(k1, p1) 4 times, p14,] twice, (k1, p1) 4 times, p12 (13).
Row 19: K12 (13), [(p1, k1) 4 times, p1, k4, (p1, k1) twice, p1, k4] twice, (p1, k1) 4 times, p1, k12 (13).
Row 20: P13 (14), [(k1, p1) 4 times, p5, (k1, p1) twice, p5] twice, (k1, p1) 4 times, p12 (13).
Row 21: As row 19.
Row 22: As row 20.
Row 23: As row 19 working inc – 79 (81) sts
Row 24: As row 20 allowing for inc sts.
Row 25: As row 19 allowing for inc sts.
Row 26: As row 18 allowing for inc sts.
Row 27: As row 17 allowing for inc sts.

Starting WS with a p row, work 5 rows St st, working inc on 32nd row *—81 (83) sts*

Row 33 (RS): Purl.
This completes the Squares Pattern.

Starting WS with a p row, cont in St st working inc on the 41st and then following 9th (7th) rows as given.

When 120 rows worked *— 99 (107) sts*, work **LARGE DIAMOND PATTERN** cont inc as set, as follows:

Row 121 (RS): K23 (27), (p1, k25) twice, p1, k23 (27).
Row 122: Starting first 22 (26) sts as follows: p2, p and inc, p19 (25), then (k1, p1, k1, p23) twice, k1, p1, k1, to last 22 (26) sts, p18, p and inc, p3 (26) *— 101 (107) sts*
Row 123: Starting first 22 (25) sts as follows: k22, (k2, k and inc, k22), then [(p1, k1) twice, p1, k21] twice, (p1, k1) twice, p1, to last 22 (25) sts k22, (k21, k and inc, k3) *—101 (109) sts*
Row 124: P21 (25), [(k1, p1) 3 times, k1, p19] twice, (k1, p1) 3 times, k1, p21 (25).
This sets the pattern for large diamonds.

Work in the same way as given for back, when 141 rows worked *—105 (113) sts*, diamonds are complete.

Now work in St st starting WS with a p row, cont inc until there are 107 (117) sts, work a further 11 rows *— 160 (162) rows*

SHAPE TOP

Row 1 (RS): BO 8 sts at the beg of the next 2 rows *—91 (101) sts*

Now dec 1 st at each end of 3rd and 3 following 3rd rows *—83 (93) sts*

Now dec 1 st at each end of following RS rows until 41 (47) sts rem.

Now dec 1 st at each end of every row until 21 (25) sts rem, BO.

SEWING UP

Work in all ends. Sew side, shoulder and sleeve seams. Set sleeves into armholes, centre of sleeve to shoulder seam.

Cloche

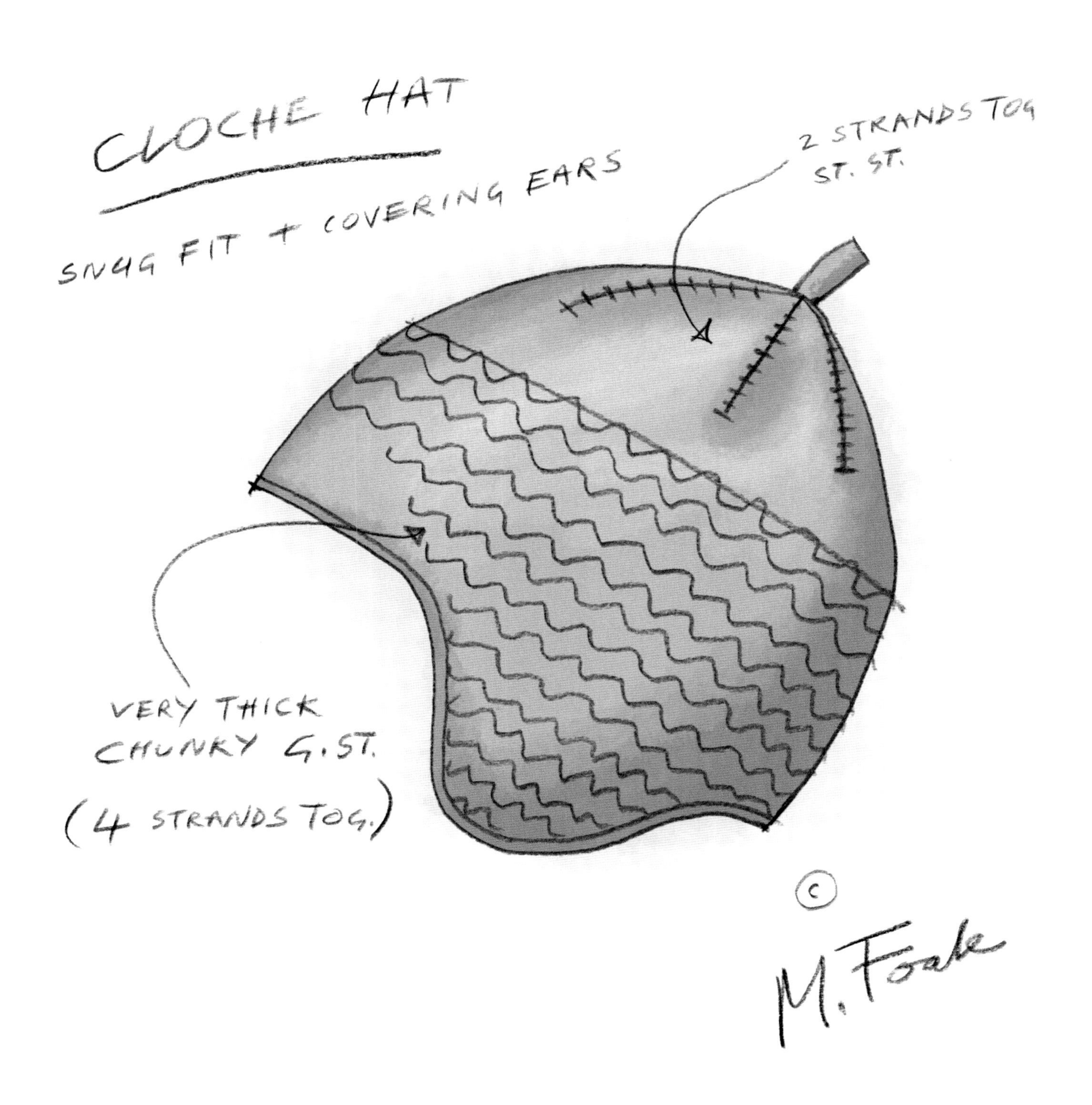

MATERIALS

- Pair size 2 (3 mm) needles
- Pair size 8 (5 mm) needles

Yarn: 150 grams **Marion Foale 3ply Wool** *—three 50g balls.* Shown in color Black #001.

GAUGE

Using 2 strands of 3ply wool together, on size 2 (3 mm) needles in St st., 26/27 sts & 37/38 rows = 4" square

BRIM

Using **size 8 (5 mm) needles** and **4 strands** of 3-ply together, CO 88 sts.

Row 1 (RS): Knit.
Row 2: K19, turn, leave rem sts at the end of the needle.

Row 3: K7, turn, leave rem sts at the end of the needle.
Row 4: K10, turn, leave rem sts at the end of the needle.
Row 5: K13, turn, leave rem sts at the end of the needle.

These last 3 rows set the pattern, cont as set working a further 3 sts each row until 12 rows worked —34 sts

Row 13: K the 34 sts.
Row 14: K the 34 sts and then next 3 sts —37 sts, turn, leave rem sts at end of needle.
Row 15: K the 37 sts.

Row 16: K the 37 sts and next 3 sts – 40 sts, turn, leave rem sts at end of the needle.
Row 17: K the 40 sts.
Row 18: K the 40 sts and next 4 sts – 44 sts, turn, leave rem sts at end of needle.
Row 19: K the 44 sts.
Row 20: K all 88 sts.
Row 21: K first 19 sts, turn, leave rem sts at the end of the needle.

Row 22: K7, turn, leave rem sts at the end of the needle.
Row 23: K10, turn, leave rem sts at the end of the needle.
Row 24: K13, turn, leave rem sts at the end of the needle.

These last 3 rows set the pattern, cont as set working a further 3 sts each row until 31st row is worked – 34 sts.

Row 32: K the 34 sts.
Row 33: K the 34 sts and the next 3 sts – 37 sts, turn, leave rem sts at the end of the needle.
Row 34: K the 37 sts.
Row 35: K the 37 sts and then the next 3 sts – 40 sts, turn, leave rem sts at the end of the needle.
Row 36: K the 40 sts.
Row 37: K the 40 sts and then next 4 sts – 44 sts, turn, leave rem sts at end of needle.
Row 38: K the 44 sts.
Row 39: K all 88 sts.

Now knit a further 15 rows, this completes the brim.

CROWN

Now using **2 strands** of 3-ply only, change to **size 2 (3 mm) needles** and cont in St st to work to crown as follows:

Row 1 (RS): * K and inc, k1, rep from * to end of row –132 sts

Cont working dec rows on the 23rd and 2 following 4th rows as follows:

Row 23: K9, (k2tog tbl, k2tog, k18) 5 times, k2tog tbl, k2tog, k9 –120 sts
Row 27: K8, (k2tog tbl, k2tog, k16) 5 times, k2tog tbl, k2tog, k8 –108 sts
Row 31: K7, (k2tog tbl, k2tog, k14) 5 times, k2tog tbl, k2tog, k7 – 96 sts
This sets the pattern.

Cont now working dec rows as set on alternate rows, thus 33rd, 35th etc. until 45 rows worked, leave the 12 sts on a thread.

SEWING UP

Work in all ends. Starting at brim (CO edge) sew edges tog, pull up the 12 sts at top of crown with yarn, pull tight to close opening, securely end off. Or make an I-cord with 4 sts using **2 strands** of 3-ply tog and **size 2 (3 mm) double ended needles,** sew firmly into crown opening.

DIAMOND

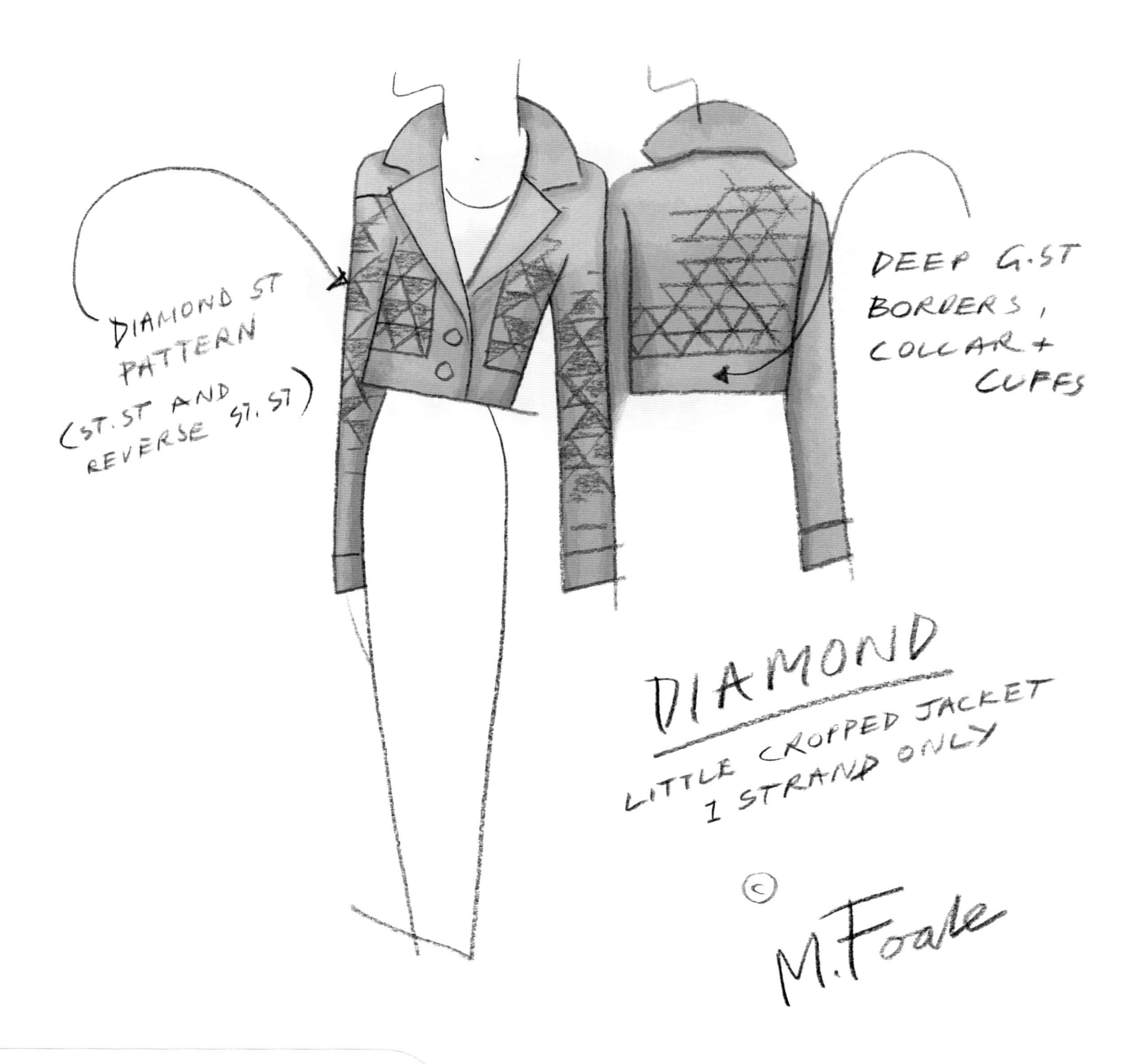

MEASUREMENTS

Actual Measurement at Bust: 38" (45½")
Finished Length: 18½" (20")
Sleeve Length —*Seam*: 16" (17½")

MATERIALS

- Pair size 0 (2 mm) needles
- Pair size 2 (2¾ mm) needles
- Two buttons, ¾" or to suit

Yarn: 450 (600) grams **Marion Foale 3ply Wool** —*9 (12) 50g balls*. Shown in colors Grape #012 and Light Olive #092.

GAUGE

On size 2 (2¾ mm) needles in St st,
34 sts & 46 rows = 4" square

BACK

Using **size 0 (2 mm) needles**, CO 141 (170) sts and work in GS (every row knit) inc 1 st at end of the 20th and 21st rows *—143 (172) sts*

When 41 rows are worked, inc as follows:

Row 42 (WS): K3 (5), * k and inc, k7, rep from * to last 4 (7) sts, k and inc, k3 (6) *—161 (193) sts*

Change to **size 2 (2¾ mm) needles** and cont in **DIAMOND PATTERN** as follows:

Row 1: (k8, p1, k7) 10 (12) times, k1.
Row 2: P1, (p7, k1, p8) 10 (12) times.
Row 3: (k7, p3, k6) 10 (12) times, k1.
Row 4: P1, (p6, k3, p7) 10 (12) times.

Thus WS rows k the k sts and p the p sts.

Row 5: (<6, p5, k5) 10 (12) times, k1.
Row 7: (<5, p7, k4) 10 (12) times, k1.
Row 9: (<4, p9, k3) 10 (12) times, k1.
Row 11: (k3, p11, k2) 10 (12) times, k1.
Row 13: (k2, p13, k1) 10 (12) times, k1.
Row 15: (k1, p15) 10 (12) times, k1.
Row 17: (p1, k15) 10 (12) times, p1.
Row 19: (p2, k13, p1) 10 (12) times, p1.
Row 21: (p3, k11, p2) 10 (12) times, p1.
Row 23: (p4, k9, p3) 10 (12) times, p1.
Row 25: (p5, k7, p4) 10 (12) times, p1.
Row 27: (p6, k5, p5) 10 (12) times, p1.
Row 29: (p7, k3, p6) 10 (12) times, p1.
Row 31: (p8, k1, p7) 10 (12) times, p1.

Row 32: As set.
These last 32 rows make the pattern.

Cont until 100 (116) rows are worked.

SHAPE ARMHOLES

Cont in pattern as set.
Row 1 (RS): BO 8 sts at the beg of this and the next row *—145 (177) sts*

Now dec 1 st at each end of the 3rd and following RS rows until 119 (145) sts rem.

Work 53 (63) rows *—80 (96) rows*

SHAPE SHOULDERS

Row 1 (RS): Cont in pattern, work to the last 6 (8) sts, turn, leave these sts on the needle.
Row 2: As row 1.

Rep these last 2 rows once more *—12 (16) sts at end of needle*

Row 5: Work to the last 7 (9) sts, turn, leave these sts on the needle.
Row 6: As row 5.

Rep these last 2 rows once more *—26 (34) sts at end of needle*

Row 9: Work to the last 8 (10) sts, turn, leave these sts on the needle.
Row 10: As row 9.
Row 11: Work the 51 (57) sts. *—34 (44) sts at end of needle*
Row 12: Work the first 34 (44) sts, and leave on ssth for shoulder seam, BO next 51 (57) sts, work rem 34 (44) sts and leave on ssth.

LEFT FRONT

Do not join yarn on front edge.
Using **size 0 (2 mm) needles**, CO 89 (105) sts and work in GS inc 1 st at the end of the 20th row *—90 (106) sts.* Cont in GS until 42 rows are worked.

Change to **size 2 ($2\frac{3}{4}$ mm) needles**, now work in **DIAMOND PATTERN**:

Row 1 (RS): (k8, p1, k7) 4 (5) times, k1 *—65 (81) sts,* turn, leave the rem 25 sts on ssth (for front band) and cont in DIAMOND PATTERN as given for Back as follows:
Row 2 *and alternate rows*: K the k sts and p the p sts.
Row 3: (k7, p3, k6) 4 (5) times, k1.
Row 5: (k6, p5, k5) 4 (5) times, k1.
This sets the pattern.

Cont until 100 (116) rows are complete.

Now measure $6\frac{1}{2}$" down from here and **mark front edge for front band**.

SHAPE ARMHOLE

Row 1 (RS): Cont in pattern as set, BO first 8 sts *—57 (73) sts.*

Now dec 1 st at armhole edge on the 3rd and following RS rows until 44 (57) sts rem, work 19 rows *—46 (52) rows.*

SHAPE NECK

Next Row (RS): *Mark front edge of this row for collar pick up.* Now dec 1 st at neck edge on this and alternate rows, when 34 (44) sts rem, work 17 (21) rows *—82 (98) rows* (2 more rows than back).

SHAPE SHOULDER

Row 1 *and alternate rows* (RS): Work as set.
Row 2: Work to last 6 (8) sts, turn, leave these sts on the needle.

Rep these last 2 rows once more.

Row 6: Work to the last 7 (9) sts, turn, leave these sts on the needle.
Row 8: As row 6.
Row 9: Work the rem 8 (10) sts.
Row 10: Work the 8 (10) sts and 26 (34) sts on the needle *— 34 (44) sts*

Leave the sts on a ssth for shoulder seam.

RIGHT FRONT

Note: Do not join yarn on front edge.

Work the same as Left Front, REVERSING *Shaping and Pattern* and working a *Buttonhole* as follows:

GS Border: Inc 1 st at the end of 21st row *—90 (106) sts*

Row 29: Work Buttonhole:
RS: K8, BO next 3 sts, k to end of row.
WS: K to last 8 sts, yo twice, k last 8 sts.
RS: K8, (k1, p1, k1 all into yo), k to end of row *—90 (106) sts*

Diamond Pattern
Row 1 (RS): K the first 25 sts, change to **size 2 ($2\frac{3}{4}$ mm) needles** and cont on rem 65 (81) sts as follows: k1, (k7, p1, k8) 4 (5) times.
Row 3: K1, (k6, p3, k7) 4 (5) times.
This sets the position of the pattern.

Shape Armhole
Measure $6\frac{1}{2}$" down and mark front edge.
Row 1 (RS): Work as set.
Row 2: BO first 8 sts, work to end of row *—57 (73) sts*

Shape Neck
RS: Mark this row at neck edge for collar pick up.

Shape Shoulder
Row 1 (RS): Work to last 6 (8) sts, turn, leave these 6 (8) sts on the needle.
Row 2 *and alternate rows*: Work as set.

Repeat the last 2 rows once more.

Row 5: Work to last 7 (9) sts, turn, leave these sts on the needle.
Row 7: As row 5.
Row 8: Work the 8 (10) sts.
Row 9: Work the 8 (10) sts and the 26 (34) sts on the needle —34 (44) sts
Row 10: Work all 34 (44) sts and leave on ssth.

SHOULDER SEAMS

Work 2 the same

RS: Using **size 2 (2¾ mm) needle,** put 34 (44) sts from the back and the same from the front onto spare needles, then place these 2 needles side by side with the wrong sides of work facing each other, now working on the right side of work k tog a st from each needle, to give 1 st on right hand needle. * k tog the next 2 sts (now 2 sts on right hand needle), then pass the first of these sts over the second. Rep from * to work rest of sts.

FRONT BANDS

Do not join yarn on front edge.

LEFT FRONT

Using **size 0 (2 mm) needles,** pick up the 25 sts on ssth and cont in GS, until work measures to marked row on front edge.

SHAPE FRONT EDGE FOR LAPEL

Now inc 1 st on this and 7 following 16th rows as follows:

RS: K to last 4 sts, k and inc into next st, k3.

When there are 33 sts, work straight until front band and lapel measures 1½" less than to marked row for shape neck, BO in k1, p1.

RIGHT FRONT

Work the same as Left, REVERSING *Shaping* and working a *Buttonhole* as given for Right Front border starting 10 rows below first inc for front edge lapel.

SHAPE FRONT EDGE LAPEL

Row 1 (RS): K2, k and inc into next st, k to end of row.

COLLAR

Use **size 0 (2 mm) needles,** starting at **marked row** for Shape Neck.

Row 1 (RS): Pick up and knit 32 (37) sts up side front to shoulder seam (approx 5 sts from every 7 rows), 51 (57) sts from BO back neck and 32 (37) sts down side front —115 (131) sts

Now cont working in GS inc 1 st at each end of the 3rd and then following 3rd rows as follows:

TOPSIDE AND UNDERSIDE

K2, k and inc into next st, k to last 4 sts, k and inc into next st, k3.

When there are 135 (151) sts, MARK EACH END FOR SEWING, work straight for 36 rows, BO in k1, p1.

SLEEVES

Work 2 the same

Using **size 0 (2 mm) needles,** CO 81 (97) sts and work 42 rows in GS.

Change to **size 2 (2¾ mm) needles** and cont in DIAMOND PATTERN as given for Back starting as follows:

Row 1 (RS): (k8, p1, k7) 5 (6) times, k1.
Row 2 *and alternate rows*: K the k sts and p the p sts.
Row 3: (k7, p3, k6) 5 (6) times, k1.
Row 5: (k6, p5, k5) 5 (6) times, k1.
This sets the position of the pattern.

Cont as set inc 1 st at each end of the 11th and then following 10th (12th) rows keeping continuing of pattern.

When there are 111 (125) sts, work 13 rows —164 (180) rows

SHAPE TOP

Row 1 (RS): BO 8 sts at the beg of the next 2 rows —95 (109) sts

Now dec 1 st at each end of the 3rd and 3 following 3rd rows until 87 (101) sts rem.

Now dec 1 st at each end of every RS row until 43 (47) sts rem.

Now dec 1 st at each end of every row until 23 (27) sts rem, BO.

SEWING UP

Work in all ends. Sew front bands to fronts eased evenly and buttons in position. Sew side seams to inc rows, leaving vent opening at hem, shoulder seams and sleeve seams. Set sleeves into armholes (centre of sleeves to shoulder seams).

CRYSTAL

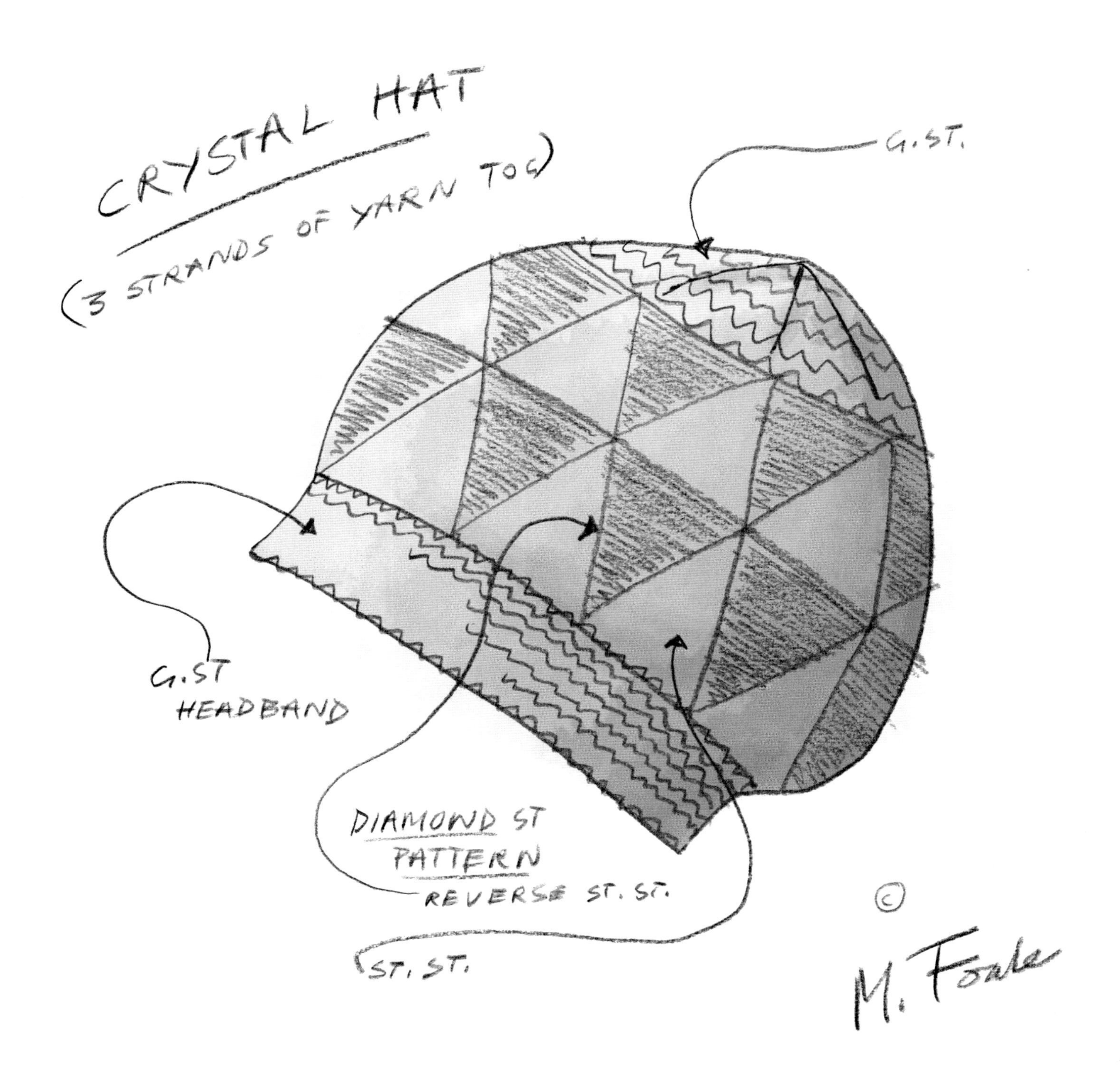

MEASUREMENTS

To fit 22" (24") circumference at head band.

MATERIALS

- Pair size 4 (3½ mm) needles
- Pair size 7 (4½ mm) needles

Yarn: 250 grams **Marion Foale 3ply Wool** —*five 50g balls*. Shown in color Cream #004.

GAUGE

Using 3 strands of 3ply wool together throughout, on size 7 (4½ mm) needles in St st, 22 sts & 31 rows = 4" square.

HEAD BAND

Using **size 4 (3½ mm) needles,** CO 96 sts. (Must stretch to 24".)

RS: Work 25 rows in GS (every row knit).

Row 26: * K and inc, k1, rep from * to end of row *—144 sts*

WORK TO CROWN

Change to **size 7 (4½ mm) needles** and work **DIAMOND PATTERN** as follows:

Row 1 (RS): (k9, p1, k8) 8 times.
Row 2: (p8, k1, p9) 8 times.
Row 3: (k8, p3, k7) 8 times.
Row 4: (p7, k3, p8) 8 times.
Row 5: (k7, p5, k6) 8 times.
Row 6: (p6, k5, p7) 8 times.
The last 3 WS rows set the pattern, thus k the k sts and p the p sts.

Row 7: (k6, p7, k5) 8 times.
Row 9: (k5, p9, k4) 8 times.
Row 11: (k4, p11, k3) 8 times.
Row 13: (k3, p13, k2) 8 times.
Row 15: (k2, p15, k1) 8 times.
Row 17: (k1, p17) 8 times.

Row 19: (p1, k17) 8 times.
Row 21: (p2, k15, p1) 8 times.
Row 23: (p3, k13, p2) 8 times.
Row 25: (p4, k11, p3) 8 times.
Row 27: (p5, k9, p4) 8 times.
Row 29: (p6, k7, p5) 8 times.
Row 31: (p7, k5, p6) 8 times.
Row 33: (p8, k3, p7) 8 times.
Row 35: (p9, k1, p8) 8 times.

Row 36: As set.

CROWN

Change to **size 4 (3½ mm) needles** and cont in GS, working a dec row on the 5th and following 4th rows as follows:

Row 5 (RS): K6, (k2tog tbl, k1, k2tog, k13) 7 times, k2tog tbl, k1, k2tog, k7 *—128 sts*

Row 9: K5, (k2tog tbl, k1, k2tog, k11) 7 times, k2tog tbl, k1, k2tog, k6 *—112 sts*

Row 13: K4, (k2tog tbl, k1, k2tog, k9) 7 times, k2tog tbl, k1, k2tog, k5 *—96 sts*

This sets the pattern.

Cont as set until 32 sts rem.

Row 35: (k2tog tbl, k2tog) 8 times *—16 sts* Leave sts on a thread.

SEWING UP

Work in all ends. Starting at CO edge, sew edges together. Pull up the 16 sts at top of crown with yarn, pull tight to close opening, securely end off.

Depending on the size of your head and knitting tension, should the hat band feel loose, thread shirring elastic through the knitting on inside of band to hold.

ISOBEL

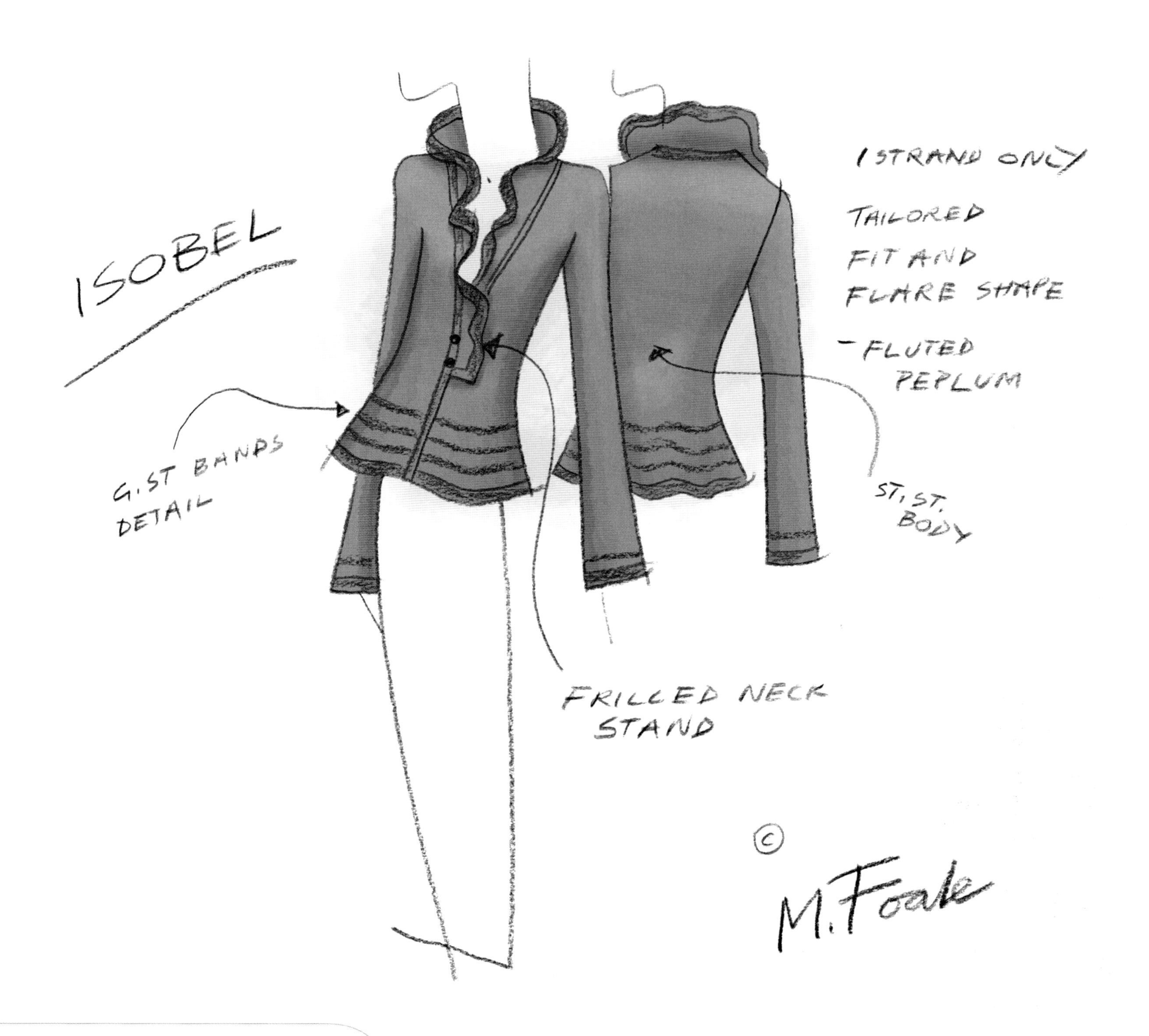

MEASUREMENTS

Actual Measurement at Bust: 34½" (39", 43")
Finished Length: 21½" (22½", 23½")
Sleeve Length —*Seam*: 17½" (17½", 17½")

MATERIALS

- Pair size 2 (2¾ mm) needles
- Pair size 1 (2¼ mm) needles
- Pair size 0 (2 mm) needles
- Two buttons, approx ¼" to ½" or to suit

Yarn: 450 (500, 600) grams **Marion Foale 3ply Wool** —9 *(10, 12) 50g balls*. Shown in colors Beige #003 and Aubergine #096.

GAUGE

On size 2 (2¾ mm) needles in St st,
34 sts & 46 rows = 4" square

BACK

Using **size 1 (2¼ mm) needles**, CO 163 (181, 199) sts. Work 12 rows GS (every row knit) for border.

Row 1 (RS): Change to **size 2 (2¾ mm) needles**, work 10 rows St st.

Change to **size 0 (2 mm) needles**, work 8 rows GS —*18 rows complete*

Change to **size 2 (2¾ mm) needles**, work 10 rows St st, *AT THE SAME TIME* working a dec row on the 19th row as follows:

Row 19 (RS): K13 (15, 17), [k2tog tbl, k1, k2tog, k14 (16, 18)] 7 times, k2tog tbl, k1, k2tog, k12 (14, 16) —*147 (165, 183) sts*

When 28 rows are complete, change to **size 0 (2 mm) needles** and work 8 rows in GS —*36 rows complete*

Change to **size 2 (2¾ mm) needles** and work 10 rows St st, *AT THE SAME TIME* working a dec row on the 37th row as follows:

Row 37: K12 (14, 16), [k2tog tbl, k1, k2tog, k12 (14, 16)] 7 times, k2tog tbl, k1, k2tog, k11 (13, 15) —*131 (149, 167) sts*

When 46 rows are complete, change to **size 0 (2 mm) needles** and work 8 rows GS.

Change to **size 2 ($2\frac{3}{4}$ mm) needles** and work 16 rows St st. *AT THE SAME TIME* on the 55th and 69th rows work dec rows as follows:

Row 55: K11 (13, 15), [k2tog tbl, k1, k2tog, k10 (12, 14)] 7 times, k2tog tbl, k1, k2tog, k10 (12, 14) *—115 (133, 151) sts*

Row 69: K10 (12, 14), [k2tog tbl, k1, k2tog, k8 (10, 12)] 7 times, k2tog tbl, k1, k2tog, k9 (11, 13) *—99 (117, 135) sts*

This completes the dec.

Work 1 row purl.

SHAPE TO ARMHOLES

Row 1 (RS): Cont in St st inc 1 st at side edge on the 21st and 3 following 16th rows, *AT THE SAME TIME* working inc darts on the 13th and 9 following 8th rows as follows:

Row 13: K28 (33, 38), k and inc into next 2 sts, k38 (46, 54), k and inc into next 2 sts, k29 (34, 39) *—103 (121, 139) sts*

Row 21: K2, k and inc into next st, k26 (31, 36), k and inc into next 2 sts, k40 (48, 56), k and inc into next 2 sts, k26 (31, 36), k and inc into next st, k3 *—109 (127, 145) sts*

Row 29: K31 (36, 41), k and inc into next 2 sts, k42 (50, 58), k and inc into next 2 sts, k32 (37, 42) *—113 (131, 149) sts*

Row 37: K2, k and inc into next st, k29 (34, 39), k and inc into next 2 sts, k44 (52, 60), k and inc into next 2 sts, k29 (34, 39), k and inc into next st, k3 *—119 (137, 155) sts*

This sets the pattern for inc rows.

When there are 139 (157, 175) sts, work straight at side edges, but cont inc darts as set for a further 2 times *—147 (165, 183) sts*

Work 15 rows *—100 rows*

SHAPE ARMHOLES

Row 1 (RS): BO 8 sts at the beg of the next 2 rows *—131 (149, 167) sts* Now dec 1 st at each end of the next and then alternate rows as follows:

RS: K3, k2tog tbl, k to last 5 sts, k2tog, k3 until 107 (121, 135) sts rem, cont straight for 49 (55, 61) rows *—74 (84, 94) rows*

SHAPE SHOULDERS, SHAPE NECK

Row 1 (RS): BO first 7 (9, 10) sts, k30 (33, 37), turn, cont on these sts dec 1 st at neck edge every row, *AT THE SAME TIME* BO 7 (9, 10) sts at the beg of the 3rd and 5th rows, work 1 row, BO rem sts. Rejoin yarn, BO centre 33 (37, 41) sts (back neck), k to end of row and work rem 37 (42, 47) sts to match, binding shoulder sts off on 2nd, 4th, 6th and 8th rows.

LEFT FRONT

Using **size 1 ($2\frac{1}{4}$ mm) needles**, CO 79 (88, 97) sts.
RS: Work 12 rows GS for border.
Row 1 (RS): Change to **size 2 ($2\frac{3}{4}$ mm) needles**, work 10 rows St st.

Change to **size 0 (2 mm) needles**, work 8 rows GS *—18 rows complete*

Change to **size 2 ($2\frac{3}{4}$ mm) needles** and work 10 rows St st, *AT THE SAME TIME* working a dec on the 19th row as follows:

Row 19 (RS): K12 (13, 14), [k2tog tbl, k1, k2tog, k14 (16, 18)] twice, k2tog tbl, k1, k2tog, k24 (28, 32) *—73 (82, 91) sts*

When 28 rows are complete, change to **size 0 (2 mm) needles** and work 8 rows in GS *—36 rows complete*

Change to **size 2 ($2\frac{3}{4}$ mm) needles** and work 10 rows St st, *AT THE SAME TIME* working a dec row on the 37th row as follows:

Row 37: K11 (12, 13), [k2tog tbl, k1, k2tog, k12 (14, 16)] twice, k2tog tbl, k1, k2tog, k23 (27, 31) *—67 (76, 85) sts*

When 46 rows are complete, change to **size 0 (2 mm) needles** and work 8 rows GS.

Change to **size 2 ($2\frac{3}{4}$ mm) needles** and work 16 rows St st, *AT THE SAME TIME* on the 55th and 69th rows work dec rows as follows:

Row 55: K10 (11, 12), [k2tog tbl, k1, k2tog, k10 (12, 14)] twice, k2tog tbl, k1, k2tog, k22 (26, 30) *—61 (70, 79) sts*

Row 69: K9 (10, 11), [k2tog tbl, k1, k2tog, k8 (10, 12)] twice, k2tog tbl, k1, k2tog, k21 (25, 29) *—55 (64, 73) sts*

Work 1 row purl.

SHAPE TO ARMHOLE

Row 1 (RS): Cont in St st inc 1 st at side edge on the 21st and 3 following 16th rows, *AT THE SAME TIME* working inc darts on the 13th and 5 following 8th rows as follows:

Row 13: K30 (35, 40), k and inc into next 2 sts, k23 (27, 31) *—57 (66, 75) sts*

Row 21: K2, k and inc into next st, k28 (33, 38), k and inc into next 2 sts, k24 (28, 32) *—60 (69, 78) sts*

Row 29: K33 (38, 43), k and inc into next 2 sts, k25 (29, 33) *—62 (71, 80) sts*

Row 37: K2, k and inc into next st, k31 (36, 41), k and inc into next 2 sts, k26 (30, 34) *—65 (74, 83) sts*

Row 45: K36 (41, 46), k and inc into next 2 sts, k27 (31, 35) *—67 (76, 85) sts*

Row 53: K2, k and inc into next st, k34 (39, 44), k and inc into next 2 sts, k28 (32, 36) *—70 (79, 88) sts*

Row 69: Work last side inc *—71 (80, 89) sts*

Work 1 row.

SHAPE NECK

Row 71 (RS): K to last 5 sts, k2tog, k3.

Now dec 1 st at neck edge every following 4th row as given, until 100 rows are worked *—63 (72, 81) sts*

SHAPE ARMHOLE

Row 1 (RS): Cont neck shape as set, *AT THE SAME TIME* BO 8 sts at the beg of the next row, now dec 1 st at armhole edge on the 3rd and then alternate rows as follows:

RS: K3, k2tog tbl, work to end of row.

When 12 (14, 16) armhole dec have been worked, cont straight at this edge, when 20 (22, 24) neck dec have been worked *—31 (36, 41) sts* Work 27 (29, 31) rows. *—74 (84, 94) rows*

SHAPE SHOULDER

RS: BO 7 (9, 10) sts at the beg of the next row, work 1 row. BO 7 (9, 10) sts at the beg of next 2 RS rows, work 1 row, BO rem sts.

RIGHT FRONT

Work the same as Left Front, REVERSING *Shaping and Pattern* as follows:

Row 19 (RS): K24 (28, 32), [k2tog tbl, k1, k2tog, k14 (16, 18)] twice, k2tog tbl, k1, k2tog, k12 (13, 14) *—73 (82, 91) sts*

Row 37: K23 (27, 31), [k2tog tbl, k1, k2tog, k12 (14, 16)] twice, k2tog tbl, k1, k2tog, k11 (12, 13) *—67 (76, 85) sts*

This sets the pattern for dec rows.

Shape to Armhole

Row 13: K22 (26, 30), k and inc into next 2 sts, k31 (36, 41) *—57 (66, 75) sts*

Row 21: K23 (27, 31), k and inc into next 2 sts, k28 (33, 38), k and inc into next st, k3 *—60 (69, 78) sts*

Row 29: K24 (28, 32), k and inc into next 2 sts, k34 (39, 44) *—62 (71, 80) sts*

Row 37: K25 (29, 33), k and inc into next 2 sts, k31 (36, 41), k and inc into next st, k3 *—65 (74, 83) sts*

This sets the pattern for inc rows.

Neck Edge Dec Rows: **RS:** K3, k2tog tbl, work to end of row.

Shape Armhole Dec Rows: **RS:** Work to last 5 sts, k2tog, k3.

FRONT BAND AND FLUTED FRILL

Use **size 0 (2 mm) needles. Row 1 (RS):** Starting at CO edge Right Front, pick up and knit 6 sts from GS band, 33 sts (7 sts from each band of 10 rows St st and 4 sts from each band 8 rows GS) 3 times, 147 (154, 161) sts up to shoulder, (approx 3 sts from every 4 rows), 6 sts down side back, 33 (37, 41) sts, from BO back neck, 6 sts up side back, and 186 (193, 200) sts as set to cast on edge *—417 (435, 453) sts*

Now work 9 rows GS, *AT THE SAME TIME,*

Row 5 (RS): WORK BUTTONHOLES: K65, yo, k2tog, k22, yo, k2tog, k to end of row.

Row 10 (WS) (DEC ROW): K70 (69, 68), k2tog, (k3, k2tog) 55 (59, 63) times, k70 (69, 68) *—361 (375, 389) sts*

Row 11 (RS): BO FOR FRONT BANDS: BO in k1, p1 (to give with knitting) first 65 sts, k231 (245, 259), BO in k1, p1 rem 65 sts.

Rejoin yarn, change to **size 2 (2¾ mm) needles** and work in St st with 3 k st at each end of every row as follows:

Row 12 (WS): K3, p to last 3 sts, k3.

Row 13: Knit.

Repeat these last 2 rows until 18 rows are complete (8 rows St st).

Row 19: Change to **size 0 (2 mm) needles,** work 8 rows GS *—26 rows in all*

Row 27: Change to **size 1 (2¼ mm) needles.** K7 (7, 8), (k and inc into next st, k1, k and inc into next st) 72 (77, 81) times, k8 (7, 8) *—375 (399, 421) sts*

Now work 29 rows in GS.

Using **size 2 (2¾ mm) needle,** BO in k1, p1 to give with knitting.

SLEEVES

WORK 2 THE SAME

Using **size 1 (2¼ mm) needles,** CO 93 (97, 99) sts. Work 12 rows GS.

Row 1 (RS): Change to **size 2 (2¾ mm) needles.** Work 10 rows St st.

Row 11: Change to **size 0 (2 mm) needles.** K4 (6, 7), (k2tog tbl, k1, k2tog, k11) 5 times, k2tog tbl, k1, k2tog, k4 (6, 7) *—81 (85, 87) sts*

Rows 12–18: Work in GS.

Rows 19–22: Change to **size 2 (2¾ mm) needles.** Work in St st.

Row 23: Change to **size 0 (2 mm) needles.** K3 (5, 6), (k2tog tbl, k1, k2tog, k9) 5 times, k2tog tbl, k1, k2tog, k3 (5, 6) *—69 (73, 75) sts*

Rows 24–30: Work in GS.

Row 31 (RS): Change to **size 2 (2¾ mm) needles,** cont in St st inc 1 st each end of the 35th and then following 9th (8th, 7th) rows as follows:

RS & WS Rows: Work 2, work and inc into next st, work to last 4 sts, work and inc into next st, work 3, until there are 105 (113, 121) sts, work 10 (11, 9) rows *—198 rows*

SHAPE TOP

BO 8 sts at the beg of the next 2 rows *—89 (97, 105) sts*

Now dec 1 st at each end of the 3rd and 3 following 3rd rows *—81 (89, 97) sts*

Now dec 1 st at each end of following RS rows until 45 (49, 53) sts rem.

Now dec 1 st at each end of every following row until 21 (25, 29) sts rem. BO.

SEWING UP

Work in all ends. Sew sice seams, shoulder seams and sleeve seams. Set sleeves into armholes (centre of sleeves to shoulder seams). Sew buttons in position. Lightly press with steam iron fluting collar edge.

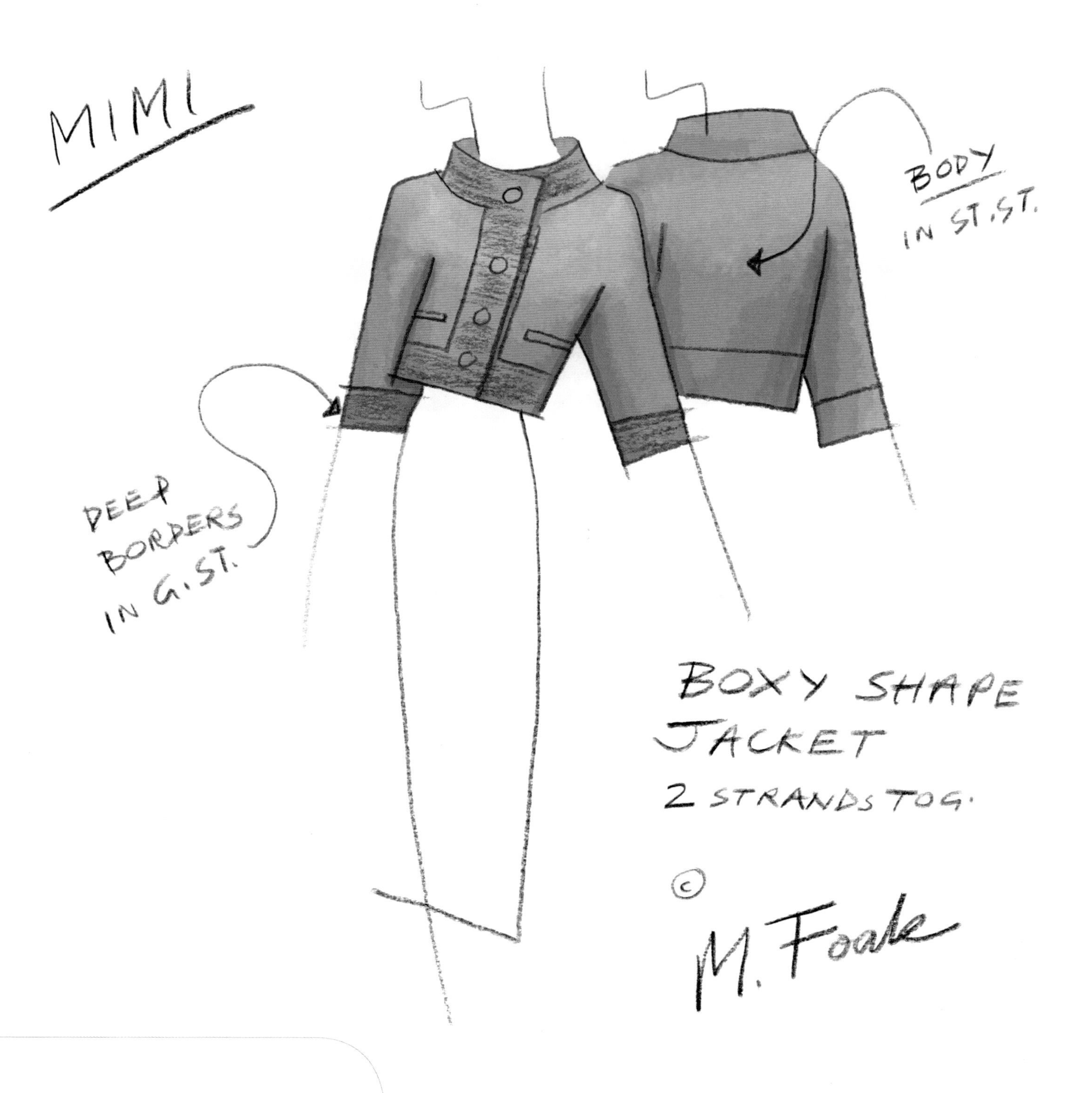

MEASUREMENTS

Actual Measurement at Bust: 35½" (39½", 43¼")
Finished Length: 19½" (20½", 21½")
Sleeve Length (from pick up): 14½" (14½", 14½")

MATERIALS

- Pair size 2 (3 mm) needles
- Pair size 5 (3¾ mm) needles
- 4 buttons, approx 1" or to suit

Yarn: 650 (700, 800) grams **Marion Foale 3ply Wool** *—13 (14, 16) 50g balls.* Shown in colors Violet #006 and Teal Green #017.

GAUGE

Using 2 strands of 3ply wool together throughout, on size 5 (3¾ mm) needles in St st, 25 sts & 34 rows = 4" square.
On size 2 (3 mm) needles in GS, 12 rows to 1".

POCKET LINING

WORK 2 THE SAME

Using **size 5 (3¾ mm) needles,** CO 27 sts and work 18 rows in St st, leave sts on a ssth.

BACK AND 2 FRONT WELTS

IN ONE PIECE—Do not join yarn at edges, but if necessary do so at side.

Using **size 2 (3 mm) needles (RS)**, CO 231 (255, 279) sts. Work in GS (every row knit), working dec on 23rd row as follows:

Row 23 (RS): K93 (102, 111), k2tog tbl, k1, k2tog, k35 (41, 47), k2tog tbl, k1, k2tog, k93 (102, 111) *—227 (251, 275) sts.*

Cont until 28 rows are worked.

DIVIDE FOR 2 FRONTS AND BACK as follows:

Row 1 (RS): K25 sts and leave on ssth for front band, change to **size 5 ($3\frac{3}{4}$ mm) needles,** k43 (49, 55) and leave on ssth for right front, k next 91 (103, 115) sts and leave on ssth for back, k43 (49, 55), turn, cont on these sts for Left Front, leaving rem 25 sts on ssth for front band.

LEFT FRONT

Row 2 (WS): Cont on the 43 (49, 55) sts in St st starting with a p row until 20 rows worked.

Row 21 (RS) PLACE POCKET LINING: K8 (11, 14), slip next 27 sts onto a ssth and in place of these k across 27 sts of pocket lining, k rem sts, cont in St st until 64 (64, 68) rows are worked.

SHAPE ARMHOLES

Row 1 (RS): Now dec 1 st at armhole edge on this and then alternate rows as follows:
RS: K3, k2tog tbl, k to end of row.

When 34 (40, 46) sts rem, (17 rows) **mark armhole edge for sleeve,** work 21 (29, 37) rows —38 (46, 54) rows

Now inc 1 st at armhole edge on the next and then 4 following 8th rows as follows:

RS: K2, k and inc, k to end of row.

When 60 (68, 72) rows are complete from start of armhole —37 (43, 49) sts, shape neck as follows:

SHAPE NECK

Next Row (RS): Cont armhole inc as set, work to last 4 (6, 8) sts, turn, leave these sts on a ssth for front neck. Now dec 1 st at neck edge on next and following rows as follows:

WS: P3, p2tog, p to end of row.
RS: Work to last 5 sts, k2tog, k3.

When 11 neck edge dec worked, work straight at this edge. When 24 (28, 32) sts rem, work 4 (4, 5) rows —76 (84, 92) rows

SHAPE SHOULDER

Row 1 (RS): Knit.
Row 2: P to last 6 (7, 8) sts, turn, leave these sts on the needle.
Row 3: K rem sts.
This sets the pattern.

Cont as set leaving a further 6 (7, 8) sts at end of needle on next 2 WS rows.

Row 8: P all 24 (28, 32) sts, leave sts on a ssth for shoulder seam.

BACK

Using **size 5 ($3\frac{3}{4}$ mm) needles,** rejoin yarn.
Row 2 (WS): Cont in St st on the 91 (103, 115) sts working a dec row on the 15th row as follows:
Row 15: K24 (27, 30), k2tog tbl, k1, k2tog, k33 (39, 45), k2tog tbl, k1, k2tog, k24 (27, 30) —87 (99, 111) sts

Now cont working an inc row on the 23rd and 5 following 8th rows as follows:

Row 23 (RS): K24 (27, 30), k and inc into next 2 sts, k34 (40, 46), k and inc into next 2 sts, k25 (28, 31) —91 (103, 115) sts
Row 31: K25 (28, 31), k and inc into next 2 sts, k36 (42, 48), k and inc into next 2 sts, k26 (29, 32) —95 (107, 119) sts.
Row 39: K26 (29, 32), k and inc into next 2 sts, k38 (44, 50), k and inc into next 2 sts, k27 (30, 33) —99 (111, 123) sts
This sets the pattern.
When there are 111 (123, 135) sts, work 1 row —64 rows

SHAPE ARMHOLES

Row 1 (RS): Now dec 1 st at each end of this and then alternate rows as follows:
RS: K3, k2tog tbl, work to last 5 sts, k2tog, k3.

When 9 armhole dec rows have been worked —93 (105, 117) sts —17 rows, **mark each end of row for sleeves,** work 21 (29, 37) rows —38 (46, 54) rows

Now inc 1 st at each end of the next and then 4 following 8th rows as follows:

RS: K2, k and inc into next st, k to last 4 sts, k and inc into next st, k3.

When there are 103 (115, 127) sts, inc is complete, work 5 rows —76 (84, 92) rows

SHAPE SHOULDERS

Row 1 (RS): K to last 6 (7, 8) sts, turn, leave these sts on the needle.
Row 2: P to last 6 (7, 8) sts, turn, leave these sts on the needle.
Row 3: K23 (26, 29), turn, leaving rem sts on the needle, cont on these sts, dec 1 st at neck edge every following row as follows:
Row 4: P2tog, p to last 12 (14, 16) sts, turn, leave these sts on the needle.
Row 5: K to last 2 sts, k2tog —15 (17, 19) sts
Row 6: P2tog, p to last 18 (21, 24) sts, turn, leave these sts on the needle.
Row 7: As 5th row —7 (8, 9) sts
Row 8: P2tog, p all sts, leave the 24 (28, 32) sts on ssth for shoulder seam.

Rejoin yarn and BO centre 45 (49, 53) sts (back neck), work rem sts to match as follows:

K to last 6 (7, 8) sts, turn, leave these sts on the needle. Cont working to match other side as follows:
Row 4: P to last 2 sts, p2tog —16 (18, 20) sts
Row 5: K2tog, k to last 6 (7, 8) sts, turn, leave these sts on the needle.
Row 6: As 4th row —8 (9, 10) sts
Row 7: K2tog, k to end of row —25 (29, 33) sts.
Row 8: P to last 2 sts, p2tog.
Leave these 24 (28, 32) sts on a ssth for shoulder seam.

RIGHT FRONT

Work the same as Left Front, REVERSING *Shaping* as follows:
Row 21 (RS): Place Pocket Lining: As given for Left Front.

Shape Armhole Dec: **RS:** K to last 5 sts, k2tog, k3.
Row 17: Mark armhole edge for sleeve.
Armhole Edge Inc Rows: (RS) K to last 4 sts, k and inc, k3.

Shape Neck: Next Row (RS): K first 4 (6, 8) sts and leave on ssth, work to end of row.

Shape Neck Dec Rows
WS: P to last 5 sts, p2tog tbl, p3.
RS: K3, k2tog tbl, work to end of row.

Shape Shoulder
Row 1 (RS): K to last 6 (7, 8) sts, turn, leave these sts on the needle.
Row 2: P rem sts.
These last 2 rows set the pattern.

Cont as set leaving a further 6 (7, 8) sts at end of needle on next 2 RS rows.
Row 7: K all 24 (28, 32) sts.
Row 8: P all sts and leave on ssth for shoulder seam.

POCKET TOP

WORK 2 THE SAME

Use **size 2 (3 mm)** needles. **Row 1 (RS):** Pick up and knit the 27 sts on ssth, work 8 rows in GS, BO in k1, p1.

FRONT BANDS

Use **size 2 (3 mm)** needles. **Do not join yarn on front edge.**

LEFT FRONT

Starting on RS, pick up the 25 sts on ssth and cont in GS until band measures 2" less than front edge to shape neck, leave sts on a ssth.

MARK BUTTON POSITIONS

The first to be started $3\frac{1}{2}$" up from CO edge, the 4th to be started on the 13th row of neck stand, and middle two to be spaced evenly.

To Work a Buttonhole
RS: K11, BO next 3 sts, k to end of row.
WS: K to last 11 sts, yo twice, k to end of row.
RS: K11, drop 1 yo, (k1, p1, k1 all into rem yo), k to end of row —25 sts

RIGHT FRONT

Starting on WS, work the same as Left working buttonholes to correspond to marked button positions, leave yarn attached to knit neck stand.

SHOULDER SEAMS

(WORKED ON RS) Using **size 5 ($3\frac{3}{4}$ mm) needles**, put 24 (28, 32) sts from the back and the same from the front onto spare needles. Place these 2 needles side by side with their wrong sides of work facing each other. Then working on RS of work, k tog a st from each needle to give 1 st on right hand needle. * K tog the next 2 sts, (now 2 sts on right-hand needle) then pass the first of these sts over the second. Repeat from * to work rest of sts.

NECK STAND

Using **size 2 (3 mm) needles**, starting Right Front Band **—Do not join yarn at front edges but at shoulder if you need to.**

Row 1 (RS): K the 25 sts, from front band, pick up and knit the 4 (6, 8) sts on ssth, 20 (20, 23) sts up side front (1 st from every row on shaping and approx 3 sts from every 4 rows along straight edge) 5 sts down side back (1 st from each row), 45 (49, 53) sts from BO back neck, 5 sts up side back, 20 (20, 23) sts down side front, 4 (6, 8) sts from ssth and 25 sts from left front band —153 (161, 175) sts

Cont in GS working a buttonhole as set, starting on the 13th row, when 32 rows are complete, BO in k1, p1.

SLEEVE

WORK 2 THE SAME

Use **size 5 ($3\frac{3}{4}$ mm) needles. Row 1:** Starting and ending on the marked rows at shape armhole, pick up and knit 83 (89, 95) sts (approx 2 sts from every 3 rows) evenly along armhole edge, (shoulder seam at centre), now cont in St st inc 1 st at each end of every following row as follows:

WS & RS Rows: Work 2 sts, work and inc into next st, work to last 4 sts, work and inc into next st, work 3 sts, *AT THE SAME TIME* working centre dec on the 7th and 13th rows as follows:

Row 7: —93 (99, 105) sts Work 44 (47, 50) sts, k2tog tbl, k1, k2tog, work 44 (47, 50) sts —93 (99, 105) sts
Row 13: —103 (109, 115) sts Work 49 (52, 55) sts, k2tog tbl, k1, k2tog, work 49 (52, 55) sts —103 (109, 115) sts

Side edge inc is complete.

Cont working side edges straight and centre dec rows on 19th and following 6th rows until 73 (79, 85) sts rem, work 1 row —104 rows.

CUFF

RS: Change to **size 2 (3 mm) needles,** cont in GS working dec rows as set on the 11th and 23rd rows —69 (75, 81) sts

When 28 rows are complete, BO in k1, p1.

SEWING UP

Work in all ends, sew pocket linings and pocket tops in position, sew front bands to fronts, eased evenly. Sew sleeve shapings to armhole shapings and then through side and sleeve seams from hem to cuff. Sew buttons in position.

GERTRUDE

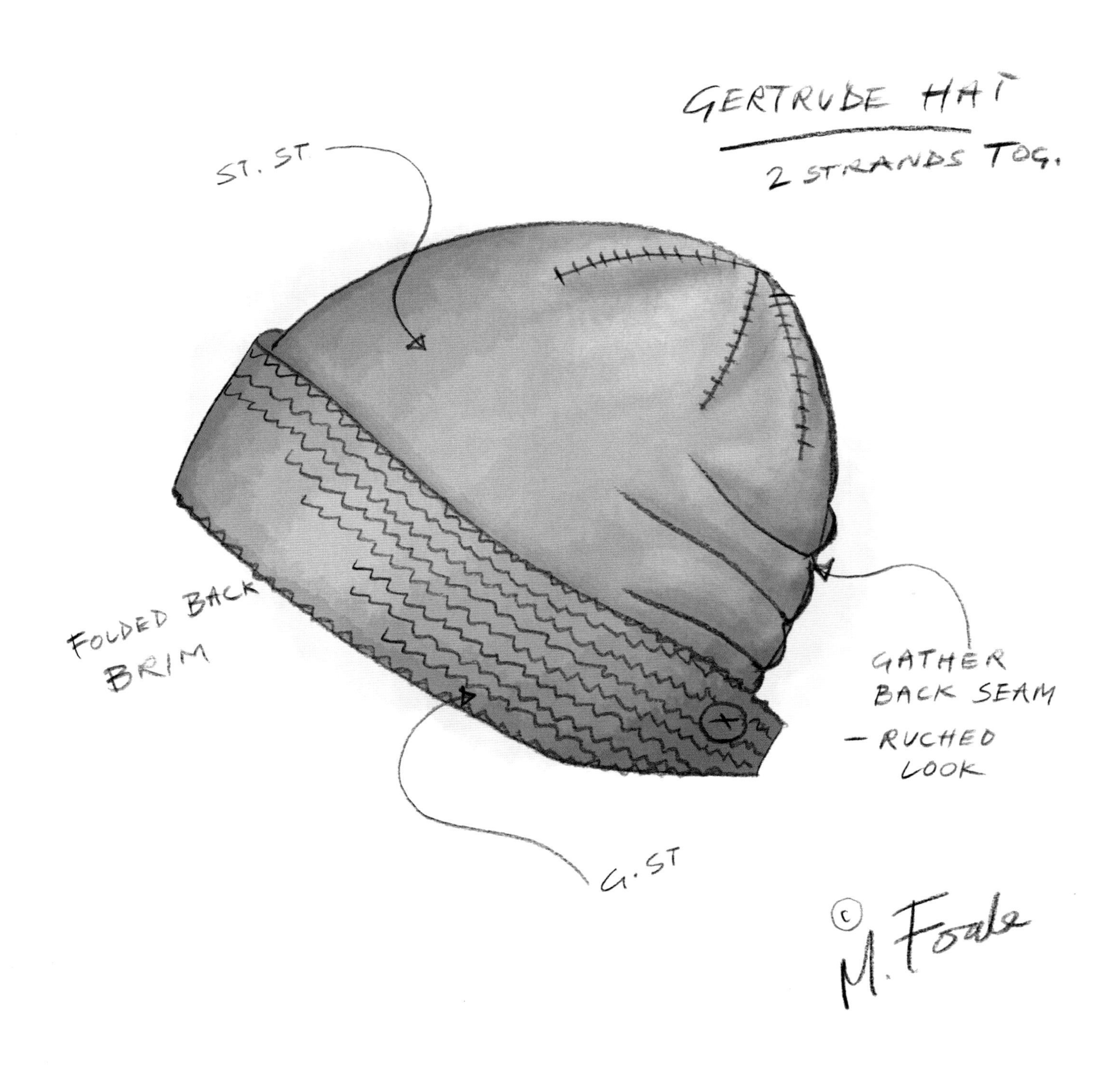

MATERIALS

- Pair size 2 (3 mm) needles
- Pair size 5 ($3\frac{3}{4}$ mm) needles
- One button, $\frac{3}{4}$" to 1" or to suit

Yarn: 150 grams **Marion Foale 3ply Wool** *—three 50g balls.* Shown in Aubergine #096.

GAUGE

Using 2 strands of 3ply wool together throughout, on size 5 ($3\frac{3}{4}$ mm) needles in St st, 25 sts & 34 rows = 4" square

BRIM

Using **size 2 (3 mm) needles,** CO 156 sts, work 1 row knit. Now cont in GS (every row knit) working shaped edges as follows:

Row 1 (TOPSIDE): K to last 30 sts, turn, leave the 30 sts at the end of the needle.
Row 2: As first row.

Now cont on rem 96 sts working a further 6 sts from the end of the needle each row as follows:

Row 3: K the 96 sts, and then 6 sts from end of needle (now 24 sts left at end). *This sets the pattern.*

When 12 rows worked, no sts rem at end of both needles —156 sts

Work straight a further 14 rows, *AT THE SAME TIME* working a buttonhole on the 19th row as follows:

Row 19 (TOPSIDE): K6, yo twice, k2tog, k to end of row.

When 26 rows are worked, shape edges as follows:

Row 27: K to last 6 sts, turn, leave the 6 sts on the needle.
This sets the pattern.

Cont as set, leaving a further 6 sts on the needle at the end of the next 9 rows (30 sts at end of each needle) —36 rows

Row 37: K the rem 96 sts, then 30 sts at end of needle —126 sts

Row 38: BO first 30 sts in k1, p1; k next 96 sts, then 30 sts at end of needle —126 sts

Row 39: BO first 30 sts in k1, p1 —96 sts

This completes the folded back brim.

WORK TO CROWN

Row 1 (RS) (TOPSIDE): Cont in GS, k the 96 sts, turn, CO 24 sts —120 sts

Row 2: K all 120 sts.

Row 3: Starting with last st, CO 24 sts, k all 144 sts.

Work a further 9 rows —12 rows

Change to **size 5 (3¾ mm) needles,** now cont in St st to work 36 rows.

CROWN

On the next row, and every 6th row 5 times more, work a dec as follows:

Row 49: K6, (k2tog tbl, k2tog, k12) 8 times, k2tog tbl, k2tog, k6 (126).

Row 55: K5, (k2tog tbl, k2tog,k10) 8 times, k2tog tbl, k2tog, k5 (108).

Row 79: K4, (k2tog tbl, k2tog, k8) 8 times, k2tog tbl, k2tog, k4 (90).

This sets the pattern for dec rows.

Cont as set until 36 sts rem.

Row 80: k2tog 18 times, leave the 18 sts on a thread.

SEWING UP

Work in all ends, starting at cast on at back edge, sew edges together. Pull up the sts at top of crown with yarn, pull tight to close opening securely, end off. Using **2 strands** of yarn together, run a thread along the seam to within 1½" of bottom edge, draw thread up to make gathered effect and secure firmly. With brim folded up, sew button in position.

POLKA

MEASUREMENTS

To Fit Bust Size: 34" (38", 42")
Actual Measurement at Bust
—*Front Only*: 17½" (19½", 21¾")
Finished Length: 26" (27," 28")
Sleeve Length —*Seam*: 17" (17", 17½")

MATERIALS

- Pair size 6 (4 mm) needles
- Pair size 2 (2¾ mm) needles
- Pair size 0 (2 mm) needles
- 5 buttons, ¾" or to suit

Yarn: 650 (750, 850) grams **Marion Foale 3ply Wool** —*13 (15, 17) 50g balls.* Shown in colors Hyacinth #032 and Donkey #095.

GAUGE

Using 1 strand only, on size 2 (2¾ mm) needles in St st, 34 sts & 46 rows = 4" square

BACK

Using **size 6 (4 mm) needles** and **3 strands** of yarn together, CO 130 (142, 154) sts.

Now work in **BUBBLE STITCH** as follows:

Rows 1 & 3 (RS): * K2, p2, rep from * to last 2 sts, k2.
Rows 2 & 4: P2, * k2, p2, rep from * to end of row.
Rows 5 & 7: * P2, k2, rep from * to last 2 sts, p2.
Rows 6 & 8: K2, * p2, k2, rep from * to end of row.
These 8 rows set the pattern.

Cont as set until 32 rows are worked.

SHAPE TO ARMHOLES

Use **size 2 (2¾ mm) needles** and **1 strand** of yarn only.
Row 1 (RS): K1 (2, 4), k and inc, k1, (k and inc, k1, k and inc) 42 (45, 48) times to last 1 (3, 4) sts, k1 (3, 4) —*215 (233, 251) sts*
Row 2: Purl.

Now work in St st with **DESIGN LINES** as follows:

Row 3: K52 (57, 62), [p3, k51 (55, 59)] twice, p3, k52 (57, 62).
Row 4 *and alternate rows*: Purl.
This sets the position of the pattern.

Cont as set working flared dec rows on the 5th and then 8 following 28th rows as follows:

Row 5: K3, k2tog tbl, k45 (50, 55), [k2tog tbl, p3, k2tog, k47 (51, 55)] twice, k2tog tbl, p3, k2tog, k45 (50, 55) k2tog, k3 —207 (225, 243) sts
Row 7: K50 (55, 60), [p3, k49 (53, 57)] twice, p3, k50 (55, 60).
This sets the position of design lines.

Row 33: K3, k2tog tbl, k43 (48, 53), [k2tog tbl, p3, k2tog, k45 (49, 53)] twice, k2tog tbl, p3, k2tog, k43 (48, 53), k2tog, k3 —199 (217, 235) sts
Row 35: K48 (53, 58), [p3, k47 (51, 55)] twice, p3, k48 (53, 58).
Row 61: K3, k2tog tbl, k41 (46, 51), [k2tog tbl, p3, k2tog, k43 (47, 51)] twice, k2tog tbl, p3, k2tog, k41 (46, 51) k2tog, k3 —191 (209, 227) sts
Row 63: K46 (51, 56), [p3, k45 (49, 53)] twice, p3, k46 (51, 56).
This sets the dec and pattern.

Cont as set until 160 rows are complete —167 (185, 203) sts

SHAPE ARMHOLE

Row 1 (RS): Cont design lines and 3 centre flared dec as set, BO 8 sts at the beg of the next 2 rows —151 (169, 187) sts

Now dec 1 st at each end of the 3rd and then alternate rows as follows:

RS: K3, k2tog tbl, work as set to last 5 sts, k2tog, k3. *AT THE SAME TIME* working flared dec on the 13th row, keeping continuity of design line detail as set with dec.

When 11 (13, 15) armhole dec have been worked cont straight working last 2 flared dec on the 41st and 69th rows —111 (125, 139) sts

Cont working design lines, work 1 (11, 21) rows —70 (80, 90) rows

SHAPE SHOULDERS, SHAPE NECK

Row 1 (RS): Work to last 6 (7, 8) sts, turn, leave these sts on the needle.
Row 2: Purl to last 6 (7, 8) sts, turn, leave these sts on the needle.
These 2 rows set the pattern.

Cont leaving a further 6 (7, 8) sts at end of needle on next 6 rows.

Row 9: Now leave a further 6 (8, 9) sts at end of needle on next 2 rows.
Row 11: K rem 51 (53, 57) sts and then 30 (36, 41) sts at the end of the needle.
Row 12: P30 (36, 41) sts and leave on ssth for shoulder seam, BO next 51 (53, 57) sts for Back Neck, p rem 30 (36, 41) sts and leave on ssth.

POCKET LINING

WORK 2 THE SAME

Using **size 2 ($2\frac{3}{4}$ mm) needles** and **1 strand** of yarn, CO 51 sts and work 50 rows in St st, leave sts on a ssth.

LEFT FRONT

Using **size 6 (4 mm) needles** and **3 strands** of yarn together, CO 50 (54, 58) sts.

Now work in **BUBBLE STITCH** as follows:

Rows 1 & 3: * p2, k2, rep from * to last 2 sts, p2.
Rows 2 & 4: K2, * p2, k2, rep from * to end of row.
Rows 5 & 7: * K2, p2, rep from * to last 2 sts, k2.
Rows 6 & 8: P2, * k2, p2, rep from * to end of row.
These 8 rows set the pattern.

Cont as set to work 32 rows in all.

SHAPE TO ARMHOLE

Use **size 2 ($2\frac{3}{4}$ mm) needles** and **1 strand** of yarn only:
Row 1 (RS): K4 (2, 0), (k and inc, k1, k and inc) 14 (16, 19) times, to last 4 (4, 1) sts, k4 ([k1, k and inc, k2], k1) —78 (87, 96) sts
Row 2: Starting with a p row, cont in St st, *AT THE SAME TIME* working side edge dec on the 5th and following 28th rows as follows:
RS: K3, k2tog tbl, k to end of row.

When 52 rows complete —76 (85, 94) sts

PLACE POCKET LINING

Row 53: K7 (11, 15), slip next 51 sts onto a ssth and in place of these k across 51 sts of pocket lining, k rem 18 (23, 28) sts.

Now cont as set working side edge dec until 160 rows are complete —72 (81, 90) sts

SHAPE ARMHOLE

Row 1 (RS): BO first 8 sts, k to end of row —64 (73, 82) sts

Now dec 1 st at armhole edge on the 3rd and then alternate rows as follows:

RS: K3, k2tog tbl, k to end of row, until 53 (60, 67) sts rem, work 13 (17, 19) rows —36 (44, 50) rows

SHAPE NECK

Next Row (RS): K to last 10 (11, 13) sts, turn, leave these sts on a ssth (front neck).

Cont on rem 43 (49, 54) sts dec 1 st on alternate rows as follows:

RS: K to last 5 sts, k2tog, k3, until 30 (36, 41) sts rem, work 9 (11, 15) rows —72 (82, 92) rows

SHAPE SHOULDER

Row 1 (RS): Knit.
Row 2: P to last 6 (7, 8) sts, turn, leave these sts on the needle.
These 2 rows set the pattern.

Cont as set leaving a further 6 (7, 8) sts at the end of the needle on next 3 WS rows.

Row 9: K the 6 (8, 9) sts.
Row 10: P the 6 (8, 9) sts and 24 (28, 32) sts at the end of the needle —30 (36, 41) sts. Leave sts on a ssth for shoulder seam.

RIGHT FRONT

Work the same as Left, **REVERSING** *Pattern, Pocket Position and Shaping* as follows:
Use **size 6 (4 mm) needles** and **3 strands** of yarn together.

Work in **BUBBLE STITCH** as follows:
Rows 1 & 3: * K2, p2, rep from * to last 2 sts, k2. **Rows 2 & 4:** P2, * k2, p2, rep from * to end of row.
Rows 5 & 7: * P2, k2, rep from * to last 2 sts, p2.
Rows 6 & 8: K2, * p2, k2, rep from * to end of row.

Shape to Armhole: Using **size 2 (2¾ mm) needles** and **1 strand** of yarn only:
Row 1 (RS): K4 (2, 0), (k and inc, k1, k and inc) 14 (16, 19) times, to last 4 (4, 1) sts, k4 ([k1, k and inc, k2], k1)
—78 (87, 96) sts

Side Edge Dec Rows **(RS):** K to last 5 sts, k2tog, k3.

Row 53: Place Pocket Lining: K18 (23, 28), slip the next 51 sts onto a ssth and in place of these k across 51 sts of pocket lining, k rem 7 (11, 15) sts.

Shape Armhole
Row 1 (RS): Work as set.
Row 2: BO first 8 sts, p to end of row —64 (73, 82) sts
DEC ROWS (RS): K to last 5 sts, k2tog, k3.

Shape Neck
RS: K first 10 (11, 13) sts and leave on ssth, k to end of row —43 (49, 54) sts
DEC ROWS (RS): K3, k2tog tbl, k to end of row.

Shape Shoulder
Row 1 (RS): K to last 6 (7, 8) sts, turn, leave these sts on the needle.
Row 2: P rem sts.
These 2 rows set the pattern.

Cont as set leaving a further 6 (7, 8) sts at the end of the needle on next 3 RS rows.

Row 8: P the 6 (8, 9) sts.
Row 9: K the 6 (8, 9) sts, then 24 (28, 32) sts at the end of the needle —30 (36, 41) sts
Row 10: P all 30 (36, 41) sts and leave on ssth.

POCKET TOP

WORK 2 THE SAME

Use **size 0 (2 mm) needles** and **1 strand** of yarn only.
RS: Pick up the 51 sts on ssth and work 13 rows in GS (every row knit). BO in k1, p1.

SHOULDER SEAMS

RS: Using **size 2 (2¾ mm) needles** and **1 strand** of yarn only, put 30 (36, 41) sts from the back and the same from the front onto spare needles. Place these 2 needles side by side with their wrong sides of work facing each other. Then working on the RS of work, k tog a st from each needle to give 1 st on right hand needle. * K tog the next 2 sts (now 2 sts on right hand needle) then pass the first of these sts over the second. Repeat from * to work rest of sts.

NECK STAND

Using **size 2 (2¾ mm) needles** and **1 strand** of yarn only:
Row 1 (RS): Starting at Right Front, pick up and knit 10 (11, 13) sts on ssth (front neck), 32 (34, 37) sts up side front (approx 5 sts from every 7 rows), 50 (52, 56) sts from BO back neck, 32 (34, 37) sts down side front and 10 (11, 13) sts on ssth —134 (142, 156) sts

Using **size 6 (4 mm) needles** and **3 strands** of yarn together,
Row 2 (WS): K2 (1, 0), (k2tog, k1, k2tog) 26 (28, 31) times to last 2 (1, 1) sts, k2 (1, 1) —82 (86, 94) sts

Now work in **BUBBLE STITCH** as follows:
Rows 3 & 5 (RS): * P2, k2, rep from * to last 2 sts, p2.
Rows 4 & 6: K2, * p2, k2, rep from * to end of row.
Rows 7 & 9: * K2, p2, rep from * to last 2 sts, k2.
Rows 8 & 10: P2, * k2, p2, rep from * to end of row.
These 8 rows set the pattern.

Cont as set until 32 rows are worked, BO in k1, p1.

FRONT BANDS

Use **size 6 (4 mm) needles** and **3 strands** of yarn together.

LEFT BAND

CO 7 sts and work in GS until band measures 2" less than front edge (from BO at top of neck stand to cast on at bottom edge), BO in k1, p1.

Mark Button Positions: The top one to be 9 rows from top, the next one to fall 5 rows lower than start of neck stand, then 3 more spaced evenly apart, the last one to fall approx level with top of pocket.

RIGHT BAND

To Make a Buttonhole (RS): K3, yo, k2tog, k2.
Work the same as Left, working buttonholes to correspond to marked button positions.

SLEEVES

WORK 2 THE SAME

Using **size 6 (4 mm) needles** and **3 strands** of yarn together,
CO 52 (56, 60) sts.

Rows 1 & 3 (RS): * K2, p2, rep from * to end of row.
Rows 2 & 4: * K2, p2, rep from * to end of row.
Rows 5 & 7: * P2, k2, rep from * to end of row.
Rows 6 & 8: * P2, k2, rep from * to end of row.
These 8 rows set the pattern.

Cont as set until 32 rows are worked.

Change to **size 2 ($2\frac{3}{4}$ mm) needles** using **1 strand** of yarn only.
Row 1 (RS): K0 (0, 2), (k and inc, k1, k and inc) 17 (18, 18) times to last 1 (2, 4) sts, k and inc ([k and inc, k1], [k2, k and inc, k1]) *—87 (93, 97) sts*

Row 2: Starting with a p row, cont in St st inc 1 st at each end of the 3rd and then following 16th (14th, 12th) rows as follows:

RS: K2, k and inc into next st, k to last 4 sts, k and inc into next st, k3.

When there are 105 (113, 121) sts, work 11 (13, 11) rows *—142 (142, 146) rows*

SHAPE TOP

Row 1 (RS): BO 8 sts at the beg of next 2 rows *—89 (97, 105) sts*

Now dec 1 st at each end of the 3rd and 3 following 3rd rows *—81 (89, 97) sts*

Now dec 1 st at each end of following RS rows until 45 (49, 53) sts rem.

Now dec 1 st at each end of every row until 21 (25, 29) sts rem, BO.

SEWING UP

Work in all ends. Sew pocket linings and pocket tops in position. Sew front bands to fronts, eased evenly and buttons in position. Sew side seams, shoulder seams and sleeve seams. Set sleeves into armholes (centre of sleeve to shoulder seam).

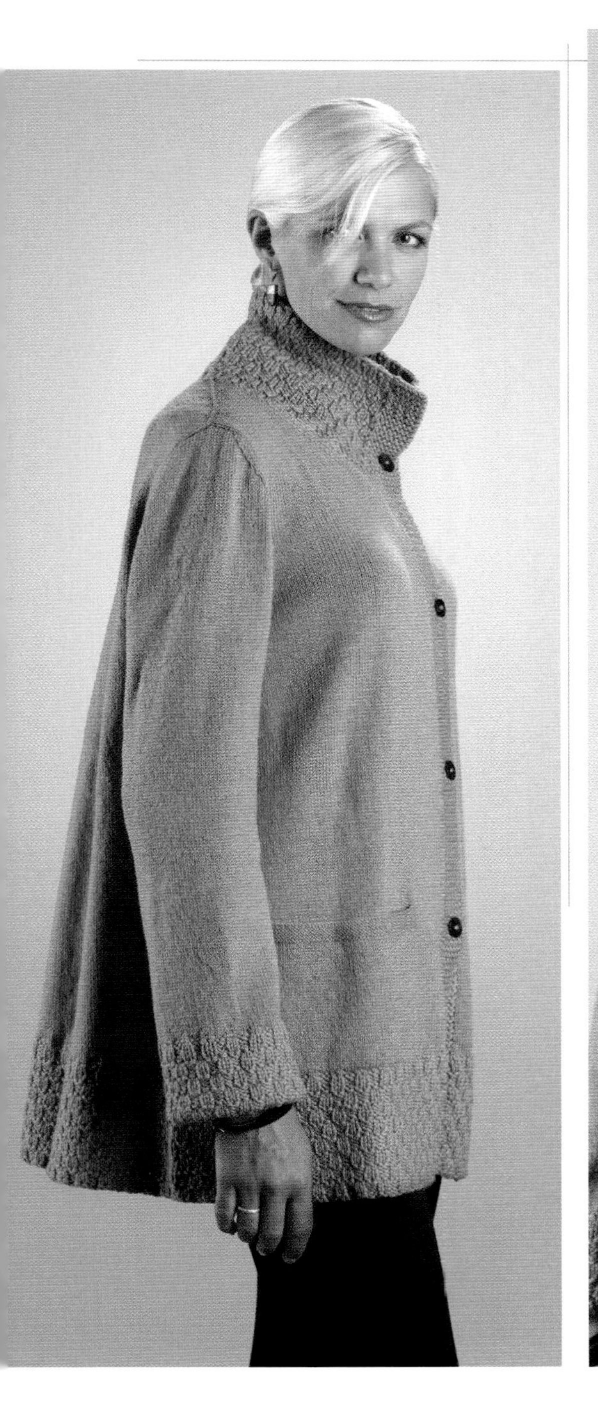

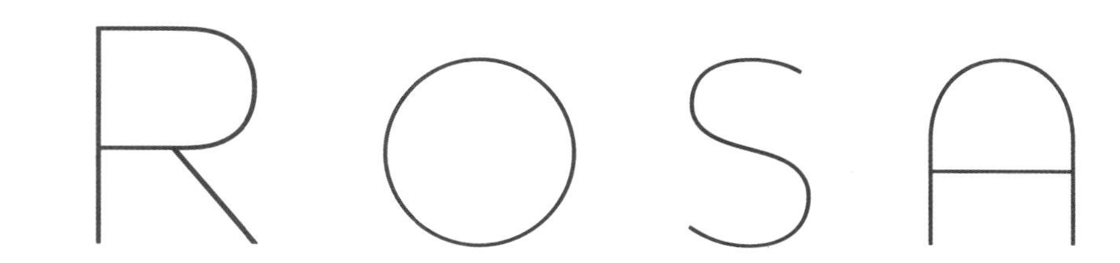

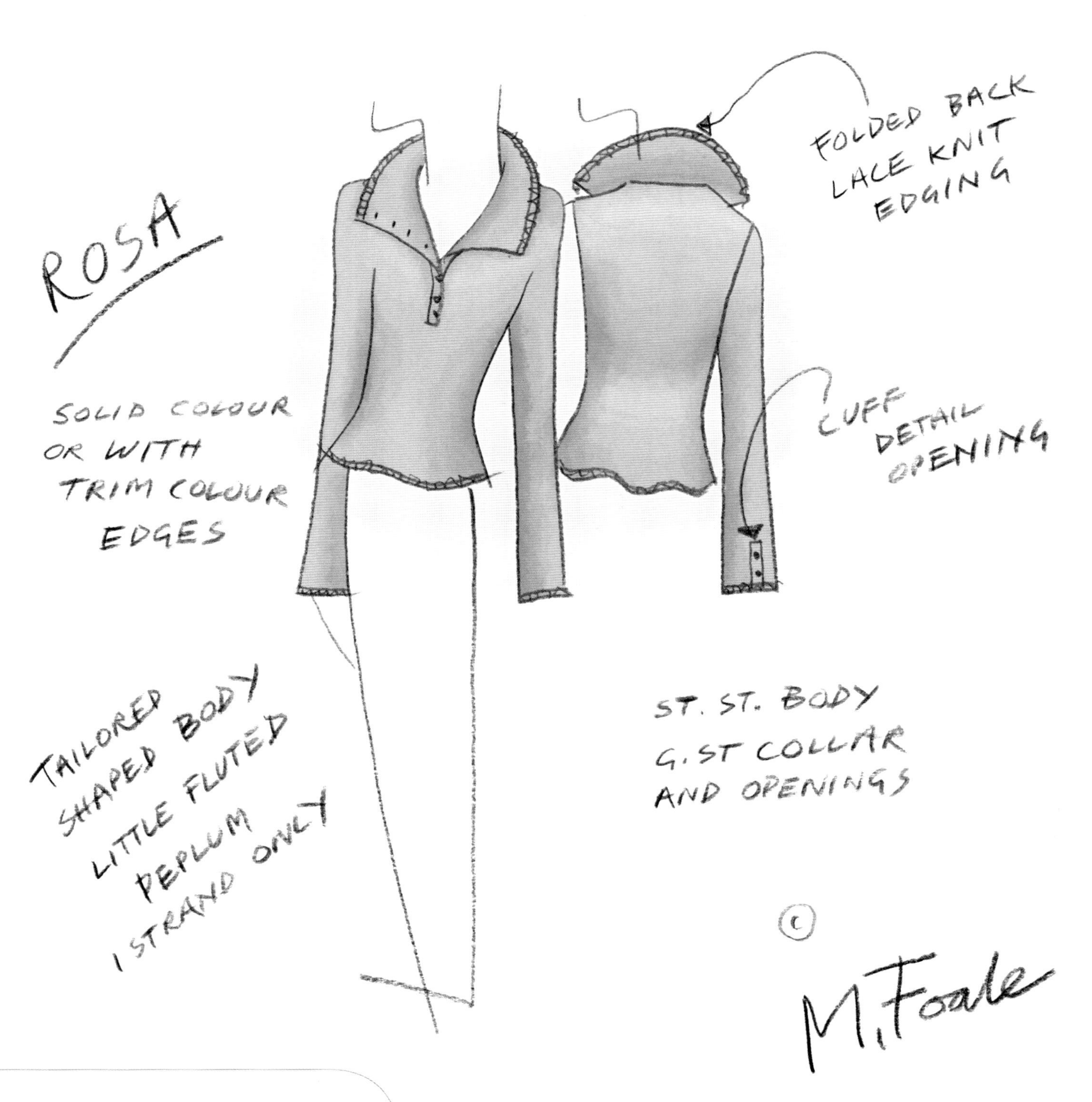

MEASUREMENTS

Actual Measurement at Chest: 34½" (39", 43")
Finished Length: 20" (21", 22")
Sleeve Length —*Seam*: 17" (17", 17")

MATERIALS

- Pair size 2 (2¾ mm) needles
- Pair size 1 (2¼ mm) needles
- Pair size 0 (2 mm) needles
- 10 buttons, ¼" to ½" or to suit

Yarn: 400 (500, 600) grams **Marion Foale 3ply Wool** —*8 (10, 12) 50g balls.* If using contrast edging, one 50g ball required in contrast colour. Shown in colors Cream #004 (MC) with Beige #003 edging (CC), and Hyacinth #032.

GAUGE

On size 2 (2¾ mm) needles in St st,
34 sts & 46 rows = 4" square

BACK

Using **Contrast Colour (CC)** and size 1 (2¼ mm) needles, CO 151 (169, 187) sts.

WORK EDGING

Row 1 (RS): Work 2 rows knit.
Row 3: K1, * yo, k2tog, rep from * to end of row.

Work 2 rows knit.

Change to **Main Colour (MC)** and size 2 (2¾ mm) needles.
Row 6 (WS): P the 151 (169, 187) sts.

SHAPE TO WAIST

Row 1 (RS): Now cont in St st working 4 dec rows as follows:

Row 13 (RS): K8 (12, 16), [k2tog tbl, k1, k2tog, k21 (23, 25)] 5 times, k2tog tbl, k1, k2tog, k8 (12, 16) *—139 (157, 175) sts.*
Row 23: K7 (11, 15), [k2tog tbl, k1, k2tog, k19 (21, 23)] 5 times, k2tog tbl, k1, k2tog, k7 (11, 15) *—127 (145, 163) sts.*

Row 33: K6 (10, 14), [k2tog tbl, k1, k2tog, k17 (19, 21)] 5 times, k2tog tbl, k1, k2tog, k6 (10, 14) *—115 (133, 151) sts*
Row 43: K5 (9, 13), [k2tog tbl, k1, k2tog, k15 (17, 19)] 5 times, k2tog tbl, k1, k2tog, k5 (9, 13) *—103 (121, 139) sts*

Work 1 row purl.

SHAPE TO ARMHOLES

Row 1 (RS): Now cont in St st working inc darts on the 15th and 10 following 8th rows as follows:
Row 15: K28 (33, 38), k and inc into next 2 sts, k42 (50, 58), k and inc into next 2 sts, k29 (34, 39) *—107 (125, 143) sts*
Row 23: K29 (34, 39), k and inc into next 2 sts, k44 (52, 60), k and inc into next 2 sts, k30 (35, 40) *—111 (129, 147) sts*
Row 31: K30 (35, 40), k and inc into next 2 sts, k46 (54, 62), k and inc into next 2 sts, k31 (36, 41) *—115 (133, 151) sts.*
This sets the pattern for inc.

When there are 147 (165, 183) sts, work 9 rows *—104 rows*

SHAPE ARMHOLES

Row 1 (RS): BO first 8 sts at the beg of the next 2 rows *—131 (149, 167) sts*

Now dec 1 st at each end of the 3rd and then alternate rows as follows:

RS: K3, k2tog tbl, k to last 5 sts, k2tog, k3.

When 109 (123, 137) sts rem, work 51 (57, 63) rows *—74 (84, 94) rows*

SHAPE SHOULDERS, SHAPE NECK

RS: BO 7 (9, 10) sts at the beg of next 6 rows. BO 9 (9, 11) sts at beg next 2 rows. BO rem 49 (51, 55) sts (back neck).

FRONT

Using **CC** and **size 1 (2¼ mm) needles**, CO 135 (153, 171) sts.

WORK EDGING

As given for Back, 1st to 5th rows inclusive.
Change to **MC** and **size 2 (2¾ mm) needles.**
Row 6 (RS): P the 135 (153, 171) sts.

SHAPE TO WAIST

Row 1 (RS): Now cont in St st working 3 dec rows as follows:
Row 15: K35 (40, 45), k2tog tbl, k1, k2tog, k55 (63, 71), k2tog tbl, k1, k2tog, k35 (40, 45) *—131 (149, 167) sts.*
Row 29: K34 (39, 44), k2tog tbl, k1, k2tog, k53 (61, 69), k2tog tbl, k1, k2tog, k34 (39, 44) *—127 (145, 163) sts*
Row 43: K33 (38, 43), k2tog tbl, k1, k2tog, k51 (59, 67), k2tog tbl, k1, k2tog, k33 (38, 43) *—123 (141, 159) sts*

Work 1 row purl.

SHAPE TO ARMHOLES

Row 1 (RS): Now cont in St st working inc darts on the 11th and 5 following 10th rows as follows:
Row 11: K33 (38, 43), k and inc into next 2 sts, k52 (60, 68), k anc inc into next 2 sts, k34 (39, 44) *—127 (145, 163) sts*
Row 21: K34 (39, 44), k and inc into next 2 sts, k54 (62, 70), k anc inc into next 2 sts, k35 (40, 45) *—131 (149, 167) sts*
Row 31: K35 (40, 45), k and inc into next 2 sts, k56 (64, 72), k and inc into next 2 sts, k36 (41, 46) *—135 (153, 171) sts*
This sets the pattern for inc.

When there are 147 (165, 183) sts, work 1 row *—62 rows*

DIVIDE FOR FRONT OPENING

Row 63 (RS): K70 (79, 88), turn, leave rem 77 (86, 95) sts on ssth, work straight 41 rows *—104 rows*

SHAPE ARMHOLE, SHAPE NECK

Row 1 (RS): BO first 8 sts, k to end of row *—62 (71, 80) sts*

Now dec 1 st at armhole edge and neck edge on 3rd and RS rows as follows:

RS: K3, k2tog tbl, k to last 5 sts, k2tog, k3.

When 11 (13, 15) armhole dec have been worked, work straight at this edge, cont neck dec as set until 30 (36, 41) sts rem, work 31 (41, 45) rows *—74 (84, 94) rows.*

SHAPE SHOULDER

RS: BO 7 (9, 10) sts at the beg of the next and 2 alternate rows, work 1 row, BO rem sts. Put centre 7 sts on a ssth for front opening, rejoin yarn and work rem 70 (79, 88) sts to match as follows:

Armhole and Neck Edge Dec Rows: (RS): K3, k2tog tbl, k to last 5 sts, k2tog, k3.

FRONT BANDS

Use **size 0 (2 mm) needles.**

RIGHT BAND

Pick up the 7 sts and work in GS (every row knit), working 3 buttonholes (the first on the 19th row, then 2 more each 20 rows apart) as follows:

To Work a Buttonhole (RS): K3, yo, k2tog, k to end of row.

Work 5 rows *—64 rows,* leave sts on a ssth.

LEFT BAND

Using **size 0 (2 mm) needles,** CO 7 sts and work 64 rows in GS, leave sts on ssth.

COLLAR

Use **size 0 (2 mm) needles. Row 1 (RS):** Working from right side of work, starting right front band k the 7 sts on ssth, then starting at first neck edge dec, pick up and knit 58 (65, 72) sts up side front to shoulder (approx 5 sts from every 7 rows), 49 (51, 55) sts from BO back neck, 58 (65, 72) sts down side front and 7 sts of left band *—179 (195, 213) sts*

Now cont in GS working buttonholes as set on 15th and 2 following 20th rows.

When 71 rows complete (16 rows worked after last buttonhole), using **CC,** work **EDGING** as follows:

Row 72 (WS): Work 2 rows knit.
Row 74: K1, *yo, k2tog, rep from * to last st, k1.

Work 2 rows knit, BO in k1, p1.

SLEEVES

RIGHT SLEEVE TOP HALF

Using **size 1 (2¼ mm)** needles and **CC**, CO 55 (57, 59) sts. Work **EDGING** as given for Back 1st to 5th rows inclusive.

Next Row (WS): Using **MC**, p the 55 (57, 59) sts.
Row 1 (RS): K48 (50, 52), turn, leaving rem 7 sts on ssth for opening, now work 37 rows in St st, leave sts on ssth.

RIGHT SLEEVE UNDERHALF

Using **size 1 (2¼ mm)** *needles* and **CC**, CO 25 (27, 29) sts. Work **EDGING** as given for Back 1st to 5th rows inclusive.

Next Row (WS): Using **MC**, p the 25 (27, 29) sts.
Row 1 (RS): K and put first 7 sts on ssth for opening, cont on rem 18 (20, 22) sts, now work 37 rows in St st, leave sts on a ssth.

WORK CUFF BANDS

Use **size 0 (2 mm)** needles and **MC.**
Top Half: Pick up the 7 sts and cont in GS working buttonholes on 19th and 39th rows as given for front, when 58 rows complete, leave sts on ssth.
Underhalf: Work the same omitting buttonholes.

JOIN TOP HALF AND UNDERHALF TOGETHER

Row 39 (RS): Change to **size 2 (2¾ mm) needles.** Starting with top half, k the 48 (50, 52) sts, now lay 7 sts of band on top of 7 sts of band for underhalf, k tog to make 7 sts, k rem 18 (20, 22) sts *—73 (77, 81) sts*

Now cont in St st inc 1 st at each end of the 41st and then every following 10th (9th, 8th) row as follows:

RS & WS Rows: Work 2, work and inc into next st, work to last 4 sts, work and inc into next st, work 3.

When there are 105 (113, 121) sts, work 9 (6, 7) rows *—200 rows*

SHAPE TOP

BO 8 sts at the beg of the next 2 rows *—89 (97, 105) sts*

Now dec 1 st at each end of the 3rd and 3 following 3rd rows until 81 (89, 97) sts rem.

Now dec 1 st at each end of RS rows until 45 (49, 53) sts rem.

Now dec 1 st at each end of every row until 21 (25, 29) sts rem, BO.

LEFT SLEEVE

Work the same as Right Sleeve, REVERSING *Opening* as follows:

Top Half: **Row 1 (RS):** K first 7 sts and leave on ssth, cont on rem 48 (50, 52) sts.

Underhalf: **Row 1 (RS):** K first 18 (20, 22) sts, turn, leave rem 7 sts on ssth.

Join Top and Underhalf Together: **Row 39 (RS):** Change to size 2 (2¾ mm) needles. Starting with under half, k the 18 (20, 22) sts, now lay 7 sts of band underneath 7 sts of band for top half, k tog to make 7 sts, k rem 48 (50, 52) sts —73 (77, 81) sts

SEWING UP

Work in all ends. Fold up edging of hem, cuffs and collar to WS and sew to back of 5th row. Sew front bands to front, eased evenly, work the same with cuff bands. Sew side, shoulder and sleeve seams. Set sleeves into armholes, centre of sleeve to shoulder seam. Sew buttons in position.

SUKIE

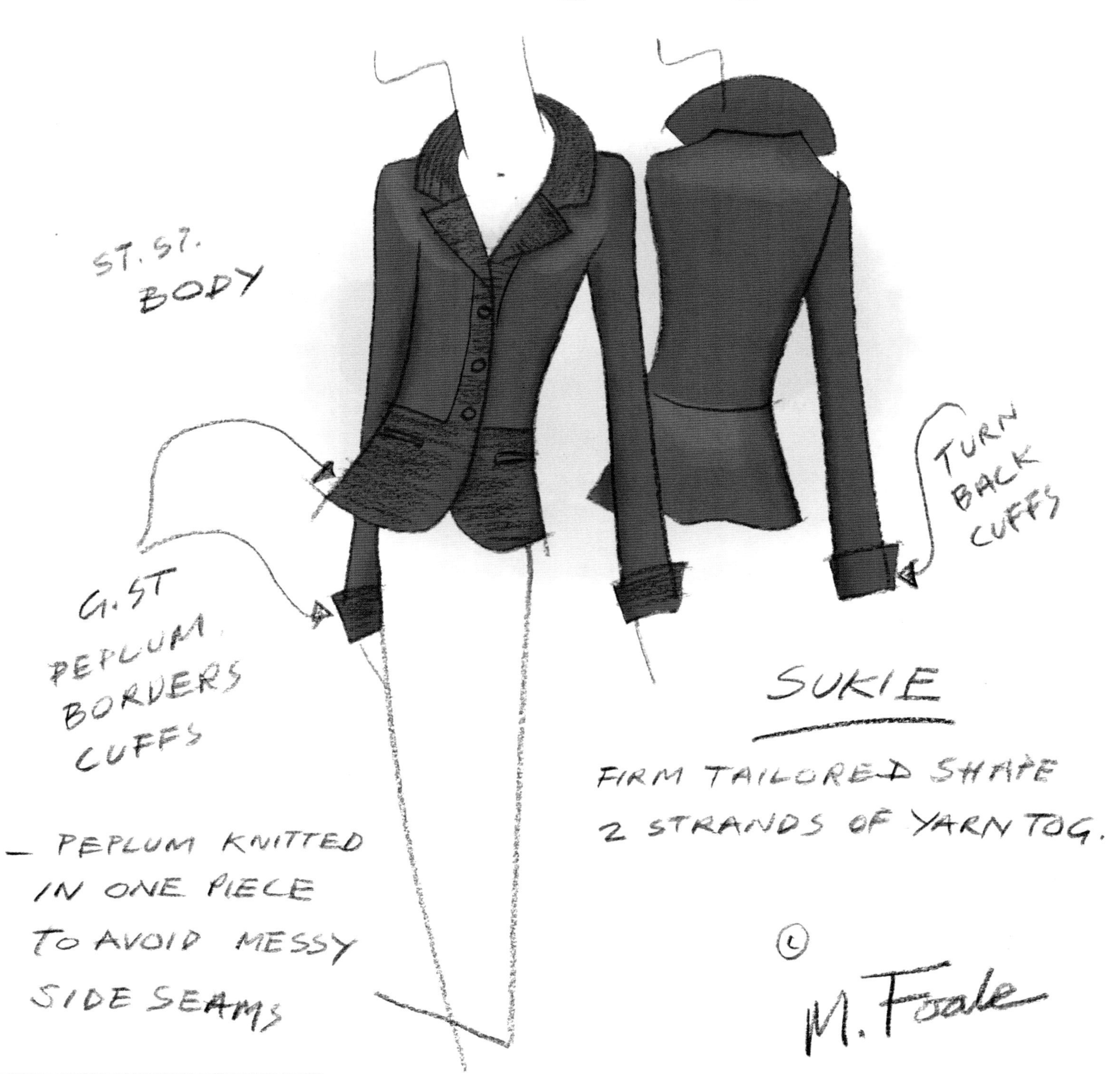

MEASUREMENTS

Actual Measurement at Chest: 35½" (39¼", 43¼")
Finished Length: 21" (22", 23")
Sleeve Length *—Seam incl. cuff:* 19¼" (19½", 19½")

MATERIALS

- Pair size 5 (3¾ mm) needles
- Pair size 3 (3¼ mm) needles
- Pair size 2 (3 mm) needles
- 3 buttons, approx ¾" or to suit

Yarn: 750 (800, 900) grams **Marion Foale 3ply Wool** *—15 (16, 18) 50g balls.* Shown in colors Dark Olive #090 and Dark Red #060.

GAUGE

Using 2 strands of 3-ply wool together throughout, in St st on size 5 (3¾ mm) needles, 25 sts & 34 rows = 4" square.
In GS on size 3 (3¼ mm) needles, 12 rows to 1".

POCKET LINING

WORK 2 THE SAME

Using **size 3 (3¼ mm) needles,** CO 27 sts. Work 40 rows in GS (every row knit), leave sts on ssth.

PEPLUM

Do not join yarn on front edges. Back and 2 fronts in one piece.

Using **size 3 (3¼ mm) needles,** CO 233 (257, 281) sts, cont in GS with curved front edges, flared dec rows on the 17th and 3 following 16th rows and placing pockets on 55th row as follows:

Row 1 (RS): Starting at right front, k and inc into first st, k to last 2 sts, k and inc, k1 *—235 (259, 283) sts*
Row 2: As 1st row *—237 (261, 285) sts*
Repeat these last 2 rows 5 more times. *(12 rows worked)*
—257 (281, 305) sts

Row 13: As 1st row *—259 (283, 307) sts*
Row 14: Knit.
These last 2 rows set the pattern.

Rep 3 more times, *AT THE SAME TIME*, working a dec row on the 17th row as follows:

Row 17 (RS): *—261 (285, 309) sts* K and inc, k13 (15, 17), [k2tog tbl, k1, k2tog, k16 (18, 20)] twice, k1, k2tog, k13 (15, 17), [k2tog tbl, k1, k2tog, k11 (12, 13)] 8 times, k2 (4, 6), k2tog tbl, k1, [k16 (18, 20), k2tog tbl, k1, k2tog] twice, k12 (14, 16), k and inc, k1 *—237 (261, 285) sts*

When 20 rows worked *—239 (263, 287) sts*
Row 21: Knit.
Row 22: As 2nd row *—241 (265, 289) sts*
Row 23: Knit.
These last 3 rows set the pattern.

Rep 3 more times. *—32 rows —247 (271, 295) sts*

Row 33: K19 (21, 23), [k2tog tbl, k1, k2tog, k14 (16, 18)] twice, k1, k2tog, k12 (14, 16), [k2tog tbl, k1, k2tog, k9 (10, 11)] 8 times, k3 (5, 7), k2tog tbl, k1, [k14 (16, 18), k2tog tbl, k1, k2tog] twice, k19 (21, 23) *—221 (245, 269) sts*
Row 35: As 1st row *—223 (247, 271) sts*
Work 3 rows knit.
These last 4 rows set the pattern.

Rep twice more. *—46 rows —227 (251, 275) sts*

Row 47: As 1st row *—229 (253, 277) sts*
Row 48: Knit.
Row 49: K22 (24, 26), [k2tog tbl, k1, k2tog, k12 (14, 16)] twice, k1, k2tog, k11 (13, 15), [k2tog tbl, k1, k2tog, k7 (8, 9)] 8 times, k4 (6, 8), k2tog tbl, k1, [k12 (14, 16), k2tog tbl, k1, k2tog] twice, k22 (24, 26) *—203 (227, 251) sts*
Row 50: Work 5 rows knit.

Row 55 (RS): PLACE POCKET LININGS: K21 (24, 27), slip next 27 sts onto a ssth and in place of these k 27 sts of pocket lining, k107 (125, 143), slip next 27 sts onto a ssth and in place of these k 27 sts of pocket lining, k21 (24, 27).
Row 56: Work 9 rows knit.
Row 65: K21 (23, 25), [k2tog tbl, k1, k2tog, k10 (12, 14)] twice, k1, k2tog tbl, k10 (12, 14), [k2tog tbl, k1, k2tog, k5 (6, 7)] 8 times, k5 (7, 9), k2tog tbl, k1, [k10 (12, 14), k2tog tbl, k1, k2tog] twice, k21 (23, 25) *—177 (201, 225) sts*

Work 1 row.

BACK

SHAPE TO ARMHOLES

Row 1 (RS): From peplum put first 52 (58, 64) sts onto a ssth for right front, using **size 5 (3¾ mm) needle,** rejoin yarn, pick up and knit next 73 (85, 97) sts, leave rem 52 (58, 64) sts on a ssth for left front.

Now cont in St st working inc darts on the 7th and 7 following 8th rows, *AT THE SAME TIME* working side inc on the 15th and 2 following 16th rows as follows:

Row 7 (RS): K20 (23, 26), k and inc into next 2 sts, k28 (34, 40), k and inc into next 2 sts, k21 (24, 27) *—77 (89, 101) sts*
Row 15: K2, k and inc into next st, k18 (21, 24), k and inc into next 2 sts, k30 (36, 42), k and inc into next 2 sts, k18 (21, 24), k and inc into next st, k3 *—83 (95, 107) sts*
Row 22: K23 (26, 29), k and inc into next 2 sts, k32 (38, 44), k and inc into next 2 sts, k24 (27, 30) *—87 (99, 111) sts*
Row 31: K2, k and inc into next st, k21 (24, 27), k and inc into next 2 sts, k34 (40, 46), k and inc into next 2 sts, k21 (24, 27), k and inc into next st, k3 *—93 (105, 117) sts*
This sets the pattern for inc.

When there are 111 (123, 135) sts, work 3 rows *—66 rows*

SHAPE ARMHOLES

Row 1 (RS): BO 6 sts at the beg of the next 2 rows *—99 (111, 123) sts*

Now dec 1 st at each end of the next and then alternate rows as follows:

RS: K3, k2tog tbl, k to last 5 sts, k2tog, k3, until 79 (89, 99) sts rem. Work 39 (45, 51) rows *—60 (68, 76) rows total.*

SHAPE SHOULDERS

BO 7 (9, 10) sts at the beg of the next 4 rows, BO 9 (9, 11) sts at the beg of next 2 rows, BO rem 33 (35, 37) sts (back neck).

LEFT FRONT

Use **size 5 (3¾ mm) needles.**

SHAPE TO ARMHOLES

Row 1 (RS): Starting from side edge, pick up and knit 41 (47, 53) sts on ssth, turn, cont on these sts leaving rem 11 sts on a ssth for border.

Cont in St st, *AT THE SAME TIME* working inc dart on the 7th and 2 following 16th rows and side inc on the 15th and 2 following 16th rows as follows:

Row 7: K28 (32, 36), k and inc into next 2 sts, k11 (13, 15) *—43 (49, 55) sts*
Row 15: K2, k and inc next st, k to end of row *—44 (50, 56) sts*
Row 23: K30 (34, 38), k and inc into next 2 sts, k12 (14, 16) *—46 (52, 58) sts*
Row 31: K2, k and inc into next st, k to end of row *—47 (53, 59) sts*
Row 39: K32 (36, 40), k and inc into next 2 sts, k13 (15, 17) *—49 (55, 61) sts*
This completes the inc dart.

Work 1 further side inc as set *—50 (56, 62) sts*

Work 19 rows *—66 rows*

Now measure down 1" and **mark front edge for front band.**

SHAPE ARMHOLE AND FRONT EDGE

Row 1 (RS): BO first 6 sts, k to last 5 sts, k2tog, k3 *—43 (49, 55) sts*

Now dec 1 st at armhole edge on the 3rd and then alternate rows and 1 st at neck edge on 4 following 4th rows as follows:

Armhole Dec Rows (RS): K3, k2tog tbl, work to end of row.
Front Edge Dec Rows (RS): Work to last 5 sts, k2tog, k3.

When 5 front edge decreases and 10 (11, 12) armhole decreases have been worked *—29 (34, 39) sts,* work 21 (25, 29) rows *—42 (48, 54) rows*

SHAPE NECK

Next Row (RS): Mark this row for collar. Now dec 1 st at neck edge on this and then 5 (6, 7) alternate rows as follows:

RS: K to last 5 sts, k2tog, k3, until 23 (27, 31) sts rem, work 7 rows *—60 (68, 76) rows total*

SHAPE SHOULDER

RS: BO 7 (9, 10) sts at the beg of the next and alternate row, work 1 row, BO rem sts.

RIGHT FRONT

Starting from front edge, work the same as Left Front, REVERSING *Shaping* as follows:

Row 1: K first 11 sts, and leave on ssth for front band. Change to **size 5 (3¾ mm) needles,** k to end of row *—41 (47, 53) sts*

Row 7 (RS): *(first inc row)* K10 (12, 14), k and inc into next 2 sts, k29 (33, 37) *—43 (49, 55) sts*

Row 15: K to last 4 sts, k and inc into next st, k3 *—44 (50, 56) sts*

This sets the pattern.

Mark Front Edge 1" below shape armhole.
Shape Armhole (RS): Work to last 5 sts, k2tog, k3.
Shape Front Edge (RS): K3, k2tog tbl, work to end of row.
Shape Neck Dec (RS): K3, k2tog tbl, k to end of row.

FRONT BANDS

Use **size 2 (3 mm) needles.**

LEFT SIDE

RS: Pick up the 11 sts on ssth and work in GS until band measures 1" less than to marked row at front edge.

SHAPE FRONT EDGE FOR LAPEL

Cont in GS inc 1 st at front edge on next and 5 following 3rd rows as follows:

Row 1 (RS): Work to last 4 sts, k and inc into next st, k3.
Row 4 (WS): K2, k and inc into next st, work to end of row.
This sets inc pattern.

When 16 rows have been worked (17 sts), cont inc on the 17th and 6 following 6th rows as given for RS. *AT THE SAME TIME*, inc 1 st at inside edge on next and 4 following 6th rows as follows:

Row 17 (RS): K2, k and inc into next st, work to end of row.

When there are 29 sts, work straight until band and lapel measures 1½" less than to marked row at shape neck, leave sts on a ssth.

Mark Button Positions: The first to be on the 3rd row (from pick up on ssth), the last to be 3 rows beneath shape front edge for lapel, and one evenly spaced between.

RIGHT SIDE

Work the same as Left, REVERSING *Shaping* and working *3 Buttonholes* to correspond to button positions.

To Work a Buttonhole (RS): K5, yo twice, k2tog, k to end of row.

Lapel Inc
RS: K2, k and inc into next st, work to end of row.
WS: Work to last 4 sts, k and inc into next st, k3.

Inside Edge Inc
RS: Work to last 4 sts, k and inc into next st, k3.

POCKET TOP

WORK 2 THE SAME

RS: Using **size 2 (3 mm) needles,** pick up the 27 sts on ssth and work 3 rows GS, BO in k1, p1.

COLLAR

Use **size 2 (3 mm) needles. Row 1 (RS):** Starting at right front border BO in k1, p1 first 19 sts, pick up and knit rem 10 sts, from marked row 18 (19, 21) sts up side front (approx 3 sts from every 4 rows), 33 (35, 37) sts from BO back neck, 18 (19, 21) sts down side front and 10 sts from ssth (Left Border), BO in k1, p1 rem 19 sts *—89 (93, 99) sts*

Rejoin yarn, now cont in GS inc 1 st at each end of the 4th and every following 4th row as follows:

WS: K2, k and inc into next st, k to last 4 sts, k and inc into next st, k3, until there are 105 (109, 115) sts.

Work 2 rows. BO in k1, p1.

SLEEVES

Work 2 the same

Using **size 3 ($3\frac{1}{4}$ mm) needles,** CO 67 (69, 73) sts.

Row 1 (RS): Cont in GS, working dec rows on the 8th and 3 following 8th rows as follows:
Row 8 (WS): K22 (22, 23), k2tog tbl, k1, k2tog, k13 (15, 17), k2tog tbl, k1, k2tog, k22 (22, 23)
—63 (65, 69) sts.
Row 16: K21 (21, 22), k2tog tbl, k1, k2tog, k11 (13, 15), k2tog tbl, k1, k2tog, k21 (21, 22)
—59 (61, 65) sts.
This sets the dec.

When 51 (53, 57) sts rem, work 16 rows
—48 rows.

Change to **size 5 ($3\frac{3}{4}$ mm) needles,** now cont in St st inc 1 st at each end of the 5th (5th, 7th) and then every following 9th (8th, 7th) rows as follows:

RS & WS Rows: Work 2, work and inc into next st, work to last 4 sts, work and inc into next st, work 3.

When there are 79 (85, 93) sts, work 8 (7, 8) rows
—130 (132, 134) rows.

SHAPE TOP

BO 6 sts at the beg of the next 2 rows
—67 (73, 81) sts.

Now dec 1 st at each end of the next and 2 following 3rd rows —61 (67, 75) sts.

Now dec 1 st at each end of following RS rows until 29 (33, 39) sts rem.

Now dec 1 st at each end of every row until 13 (15, 19) sts rem, BO.

SEWING UP

Work in all ends, sew pocket linings and pocket tops in position. Sew front bands to fronts, eased evenly and buttons in position. Sew side seams, shoulder seams and sleeve seams (sewing GS cuff on the right side for fold up), then set sleeves into armholes (centre of sleeves to shoulder seams).

SCARF, STOLE & WRAP

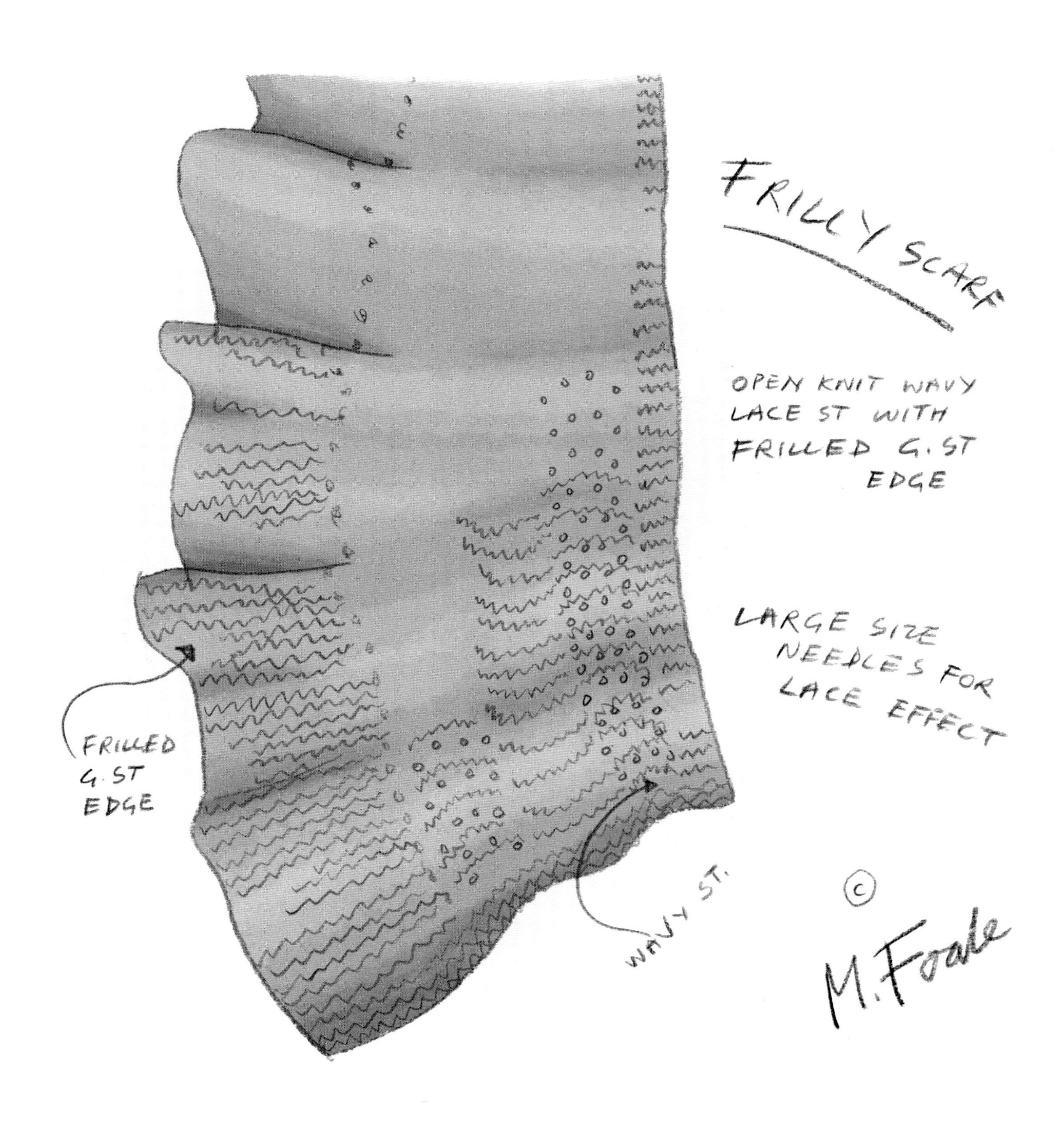

Lucy Scarf

MEASUREMENTS

Approx length: 33"
Approx width: 7"

MATERIALS

- One size 8 (5 mm) needle
- Pair size 6 (4 mm) needles

Yarn: 150 grams **Marion Foale 3ply Wool** —*three 50g balls.* Shown in color Violet #006.

Using **size 6 (4 mm) needles,** CO 44 sts. Work 8 rows GS (every row knit).

Now cont in **WAVY PATTERN with FLUTED EDGE** as follows:

Row 1 (RS): K4, k2tog twice, (yo, k1) 4 times, k2tog 4 times, (yo, k1) 4 times, k2tog twice, k16.
Row 2: K16, turn.
Row 3: K the 16 sts.
Row 4: K the 16 sts, then rem 28 sts —*44 sts*
Row 5: K all 44 sts.
Row 6: As row 2.
Row 7: As row 3.
Row 8: As row 4.
These last 8 rows make the pattern.

Cont repeating these 8 rows until work measures 32" (*at short edge not frill edge*, ending on a 1st row).

Work 7 rows knit.

Using a **size 8 (5 mm) needle,** BO in k1, p1.

FINISHING

Sew in all ends, lightly press with steam iron, fluting GS frilly edge.

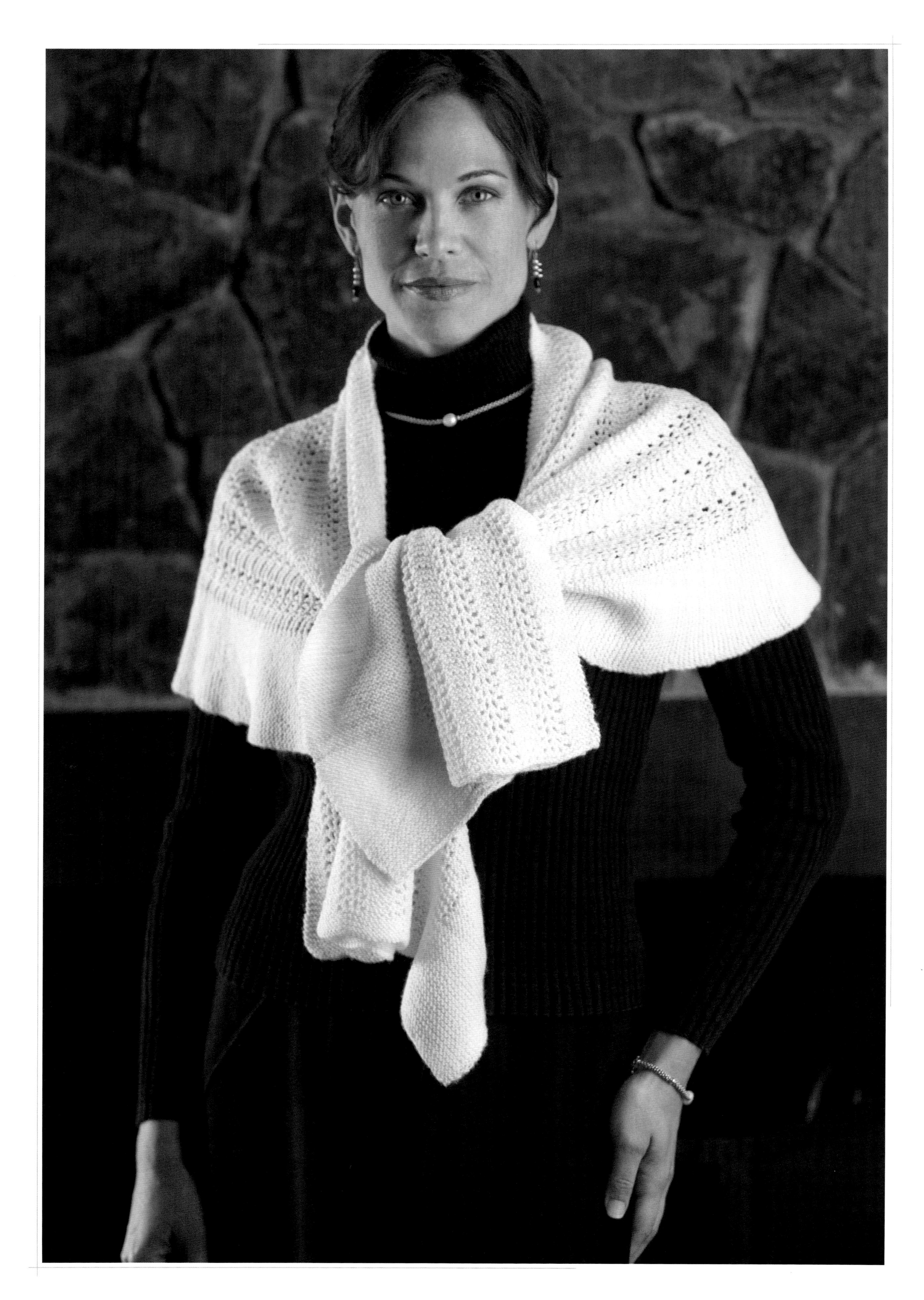

Lucy Stole

Measurements

Approx length: 60"
Approx width: $20\frac{1}{2}$"

Materials

- One size 8 (5 mm) needle
- Pair size 6 (4 mm) needles

Yarn: 450 grams **Marion Foale 3ply Wool** —*nine 50g balls.* Shown in color Cream #004.

Using **size 6 (4 mm) needles,** CO 124 sts. Work 8 rows GS (every row knit).

Now cont in **WAVY PATTERN with FLUTED EDGE** as follows:

Row 1 (RS): K4, k2tog twice, [(yo, k1) 4 times, k2tog 4 times] 7 times, (yo, k1) 4 times, k2tog twice, k24.
Row 2: K24, turn.
Row 3: K the 24 sts.
Row 4: K the 24 sts, then rem sts —*124 sts.*
Row 5: K all 124 sts.
Row 6: As row 2.
Row 7: As row 3.
Row 8: As row 4.
These last 8 rows make the pattern.

Cont repeating these 8 rows until work measures 60" (*at short edge not frill edge*, ending on a 1st row).

Work 7 rows knit.

Using a **size 8 (5 mm) needle,** BO in k1, p1.

FINISHING

Sew in all ends, lightly press with steam iron, fluting GS frilly edge.

Lucy Wrap

Measurements

Approx length: 80"
Approx width: 30½"

Materials

- One size 8 (5 mm) needle
- Pair size 6 (4 mm) needles

Yarn: 900 grams **Marion Foale 3ply Wool** —*eighteen 50g balls.* Shown in color Aubergine #096.

Using **size 6 (4mm) needles,** CO 208 sts. Work 8 rows GS (every row knit).

Now cont in **WAVY PATTERN** with **FLUTED EDGE** as follows:

Row 1 (RS): K4, k2tog twice, [(yo, k1) 4 times, k2tog 4 times] 14 times, (yo, k1) 4 times, k2 tog twice, k24.
Row 2: K24, turn.
Row 3: K the 24 sts.
Row 4: K the 24 sts, then rem sts —208 sts
Row 5: K all 208 sts.
Row 6: As row 2.
Row 7: As row 3.
Row 8: As row 4.
These last 8 rows make the pattern.

Cont repeating these 8 rows until work measures 80" (*at short edge not frill edge*, ending on a 1st row).

Work 7 rows knit.

Using a **size 8 (5 mm) needle,** BO in k1, p1.

FINISHING

Sew in all ends, lightly press with steam iron, fluting GS frilly edge.

HINTS

GAUGE

Most sizing problems are due to inaccurate gauge (tension). It is absolutely essential that your tension is correct so please always knit a tension square before starting. The correct tension for each garment is given in the instructions. If necessary, change to a larger or a smaller needle.

NEEDLE SIZE

Whenever possible, use exact metric sizes to obtain correct tension. US sizes have been given as a reference to the metric size, but, for instance, in the case of size US 2 needles, some patterns require a $2\frac{3}{4}$ mm needle and others require a 3 mm needle.

SIZES

The first size given is the smallest. Larger sizes are shown in parenthesis.

JOINING YARN

Never join yarn in the middle of a row, it always shows and can easily come apart. Instead, join yarn at the beginning of a row unless otherwise instructed.

MAKING UP

When sewing up each garment it is best to use the yarn it was knitted in. Using a tapestry needle, oversew or back stitch seams together wherever suitable. Watch that you don't sew the seams too tightly —they should be as relaxed as the knitting. Make sure that all ends of seams are very securely finished.

PRESSING

Always sew the garment completely together and then press on the wrong side of the work using a steam iron on the appropriate setting. Take great care not to over-press. A good finish to a knitted garment makes it look professionally made.

WASHING OR DRY CLEANING

Please follow the instructions on the ball band or packaging.

CASTING ON

Preferred method —cable as follows: Make a slip knot and place on left hand needle through loop as if to knit, wrap yarn around right hand needle and pull loop through, twist and place on left hand needle. * Insert right hand needle between 1st and 2nd sts on left hand needle, wrap yarn around right hand needle and pull loop through, twist and place on left hand needle, repeat from *.

Yarn quantities are approximate as they are based on average requirements.

ABBREVIATIONS

beg	beginning
BO	bind off
CC	contrast color
CO	cast on
cont	continue
dec	decrease, decreasing
GS	garter stitch
inc	increase, increasing (k into front and back)
k	knit
k1b	knit 1 stitch through back loop
k2tog	knit 2 stitches together
MC	main color
p	purl
p2tog	purl 2 stitches together
rem	remain, remaining
rep	repeat
RS	right side facing
ssth	spare stitch holder
st(s)	stitch(es)
St st	stockinette stitch
tbl	through back of loop
tog	together
WS	wrong side facing
yo	yarn over

Editor David Codling

Photography Kathryn Martin

Graphic Design & Photo Editing Eric Youngquist

Garments Modeled by Sherri Siegel and Catharina Aiello

Makeup & Hair Stylist Kira Lee

Clothing Stylist Betsy Westman

Location Thanks Nancy Denkin

Color Reproduction & Printing Regent Publishing Services

Marion Foale 3ply Wool Yarn Distributed by www.marionfoaleknitting.com

Published & Distributed by Unicorn Books and Crafts, Inc. www.unicornbooks.com

Printed in China.

ISBN 978-1-893063-24-2

10 9 8 7 6 5 4 3 2 1